Crossing Lake Michigan in a Bathtub

Crossing Lake Michigan in a Bathtub

A True Story

By Vic Jackson

Lakes & Peaks Publishing

Published by Lakes & Peaks Publishing
2377 Seminole Dr. Okemos, Michigan 48864

Written by Vic Jackson
Designed by Karen Jackson
Front Cover Photo by Greg Hiscock
Back Cover Photo 1 & 2 by Paul Zarkovich
Back-Cover Photo 3 by United Press International Photo

Printed in USA
ISBN 978-0-578-52682-9

Dedication

Dedicated to the brave women and men of the United States Coast Guard and to Amateur Radio Operators around the world who provide emergency communications when all else fails, sometimes at great peril to their lives.

The motto of the United States Coast Guard is Semper Paratus or Always Ready (the traditional translation of the Latin). Today's more down-to-earth Coast Guard sailors have a slightly different translation: "You have to go out, but you don't have to come back."

Maritime history is crowded with stories of Coast Guard personnel who were dispatched to the rescue but never returned. The personnel of the U.S. Coast Guard Station Ludington, Michigan did go out one day and rescue me and my bathtub from Lake Michigan, and all did come safely back on that occasion. I am forever grateful and humbled in their presence.

During natural disasters and national emergencies, amateur (ham) radio operators provide essential communications services that save thousands of lives. I am forever indebted to my fellow ham operators (Fred Richter W8VTM Ludington, Michigan, and Tim Selmer WA9SRW, Kewaunee, Wisconsin) who, through their relay communications to onshore and marine rescuers, ensured both my rescue and my eventual success in crossing Lake Michigan.

Table of Contents

FOREWORD

Periodically, over the years, while cleaning or rearranging a storage cabinet in the basement, I stumble across a well-worn cardboard box that hides a collection of bizarre items: a large metallic replica of a key on a faded blue ribbon bearing the words "Manitowoc Wis" in raised letters. This strange doodad, over a foot long and weighing nearly a pound, was obviously meant to be displayed trophy style on an office wall. The box also contains an impressive but worn magnetic compass from an airplane of World War II vintage. It's mounted on a panel of scrap aluminum. Joining these items is a large, transistor portable radio (likely 1960s vintage) that long ago corroded beyond repair.

Wondering how and why I possess these seemingly useless relics triggers a flood of memories and raw emotions from times past. Vivid images of roiling green water, white-capped waves, a tiny boat and a brush with death race through my brain. I catch my breath as I realize this unassuming box of junk, my souvenirs of a foolhardy venture, carries one whale of a true story—one I am alive to tell in this saga of a bathtub mariner. In fact, these worn and rusty artifacts saved my life.

At some time or another, a storyteller has probably said to you, "You won't believe this story," and then proceeded to describe an event or circumstance so ridiculous you think it's either a lie or a fantasy. But then someone else suggests that it's so outlandish no one could ever have made it up.

Over the last 50 years, since boxing up and stowing these relics, I've answered the same question and heard the same disbelief a zillion times:

"Why in the world did you—why would anyone—attempt to cross Lake Michigan in a bathtub?"

My short answer: "To win a $5 bet with my boss!"

"Did you use a real bathtub?"

"Yep. It was a real, honest-to-goodness Kohler cast-iron bathtub, and it was heavier than hell."

This book is a confession of sorts, more than anything, to explain the truth about a really weird and very personal story – a story that vaulted me into an odyssey of failure and success, notoriety and fame, with redemption as my only true reward. And it happened entirely by chance!

Acknowledgements

A Million Thanks to the Crew of Modern Volunteers
Who Made this Story Into a Book

To Senior Editor Gail Braverman who made a mad mangle of words into a readable narrative, and for her magical, mystical talents in professional editing and for her advice to a novice writer.

To Professor Nancy DeJoy at Michigan State University for her extraordinary help with final editing, layout, and publishing issues and for spotting wasted spaces and errant conjunctive adverbs.

To Karen Jackson who is, without doubt, the reason you are able to read this book, for her outstanding book cover design and motivational efforts directed at a neophyte author, and for doing countless, seemingly impossible but necessary tasks required to publish a book, and who said, for about 40 years, "You need an editor."

To Valerie Jackson who read early drafts of this story, helped immensely with questions to be answered, and said "You need an editor."

To Ron Roush who read very early drafts of this story, suggested that writing was not one of my talents, and said "You need an editor."

The adventure described in this narrative would not have been possible without the people and organizations listed below, as well as those generous souls whose identity I have not been able to ascertain. These are true friends and family who will always have my heartfelt thanks and undying gratitude.

The names, titles and affiliations for the people and organizations below are listed in alphabetical order and are as they were in 1969.

•The Ann Arbor Railroad Carferry Service Frankfort Michigan
•Fred Behnke, Service Manager, Troup Electronics, Jackson, Michigan.
•Arthur Breece, Papermaker, Packaging Corporation of America, Eastlake, Michigan.
•June "Gail" Breece, Homemaker, Eastlake, Michigan.
•Richard Cahill, Cahill Answering Service, Lansing, Michigan.
•The Chesapeake and Ohio Railway Carferry Service Ludington, Michigan.
•Custom Electronics, Capital City Airport, Lansing, Michigan.
•Fielding Central Realty of Ludington Michigan.
•Gordon Forgar, Co-Owner, Forgars Boat City of Lansing.
•Polly Forger, Co-Owner, Forgars Boat City of Lansing.
•Forgars Boat City of Lansing.
•Lee Gillette, Owner, Gillette Sand and Gravel, East Lansing, Michigan.
•Goodson-Todman Productions, New York, N.Y.
•Earl "Ed" Grable, WB8CET, Owner, Grable and Sons Metal Products, Dimondale, Michigan.
•Grable and Sons Metal Products, Dimondale, Michigan.

•Gerald Graves, Mayor of the City of Lansing, Michigan.
•David Haddrill, Student, Michigan State University
•Dave Hanson, Reporter, Lansing State Journal, Lansing, Michigan.
•Gerald Heslipen, Captain, Chesapeake and Ohio Railway Carferry Service, Ludington, Michigan.
•Don Hewson, WB8CEU, Lieutenant, East Lansing Police Department, E.L. Michigan.
•Greg Hiscock, WA8DLI, Service Technician, Troup Electronics, Jackson, Michigan.
•James Holcomb, Civil Defense Director, City of Lansing, Michigan WA8KZY
•Don Jackson Sr. Superintendent of Operations and Maintenance of Way, Ludington and Northern Railway, Ludington, Michigan.
•John Krey, Mayor of the City of Manitowoc, Wisconsin.
•Willard Lake, Ludington, Michigan.
•Ludington Daily News, Ludington, Michigan.
•The City of Lansing, Michigan.
•The City of Ludington, Michigan.
•The City of Manitowoc, Wisconsin.
•Brian Monaghan, Electronics Service Technician, Grand Ledge, Michigan. (Now KC8QWJ)
•Charles Ogle, Owner, Custom Electronics, Lansing, Michigan. (Now K4IRH)
•Fred Richter W8VTM, Amateur Radio Operator, Ludington, Michigan.
•Rita Rice, Reporter, Lansing State Journal, Lansing Michigan.
•Tim Selner WA9SRW, Amateur Radio Operator, Kewaunee, Wisconsin.

•Roger Simmer, Employee, Diamond Reo Manufacturing, Lansing, Michigan.
•Troup Electronics, Jackson, Michigan.
•Everett Troup, W8BQA, Owner and Founder, Troup Electronics, Jackson, Michigan.
•United Press International, New York, N.Y.
•US Coast Guard Station, Ludington, Michigan.
•US Coast Guard Station, Manitowoc, Wisconsin

"Your time is limited, so don't waste it living someone else's life. Don't be trapped by dogma-which is living with the results of other people's thinking. Don't let the noise of others' opinions drown out your own inner voice. And most important, have the courage to follow your heart and intuition. They somehow already know what you truly want to become. Everything else is secondary."

Steve Jobs
U.S. computer engineer & industrialist (1955 – 2011)
and father of the iPhone.

"On a rare occasion, the great waters of Michigami will allow an unenlightened mariner the extreme luxury of a second chance. She can be as kindly as a warm summer day and as beautiful as the dunes of Sleeping Bear, but the shining waters of Lake Michigan hold great contempt for nautical fools and careless sailors."

A cautionary observation by Vic Jackson,
who has been there and done that.

1

Seconds from Disaster

The summer of 1969 was unusual in many ways. Astronauts were walking on the moon, U.S. soldiers were dying in Vietnam, and baby boomers were rocking in Woodstock's muddy fields. Meanwhile, in Michigan a 31-year-old communications technician launched a bizarre watercraft into the fifth largest lake in the world to attempt a seemingly impossible voyage.

Lake Michigan is 307 miles long, 118 miles at its widest, and averages 279 feet deep. On rare occasions, it freezes over completely in winter. And in late fall it whips up gigantic waves as dangerous as any in the world for boats of all sizes.

Yet there I was, on Saturday, July 5, 1969, four miles from land on Lake Michigan in a bathtub. It was a crisp, sunny day on the big lake with a northwest wind whipping up a surfer's delight of large waves. As my strange vessel plowed through the top of another wave, cascading water inundated the whole front end. "If this thing capsizes," I thought, "I could easily get trapped under water." It felt like I was riding a bucking bull from hell in a rodeo. Foaming-at-the-mouth waves tossed me up and down, back and forth, jarring me to the bone. Semi-reclined on my back as if taking a bath, I faced the outboard motor in the rear, away from my direction of travel.

With every ride up the front of a surging wave, the tub would shudder from the onslaught, snap into a sharp drop, and nose-dive into the next trough. This stomach-wrenching fall ended when the tub and I hit bottom in the churning green canyon—water just inches from my body on all sides. Within a second or two, my rig would begin its rise again on the next swell, first slowly, then faster and faster as my back again approached a foaming, white wall. Unable to see ahead intensified my fear that any second a monster wave would completely swallow me or wash away my lifeline communications. I knew I had to call for help. As the tub slammed into the bottom of the next wave, I grabbed for the microphone on the two-way radio:

"W8VTM this is W8BLP marine mobile, do you copy, Fred?"

No answer.

I called again....

....SILENCE

Desperation and terror pounded in my head. My life depended on a homespun collection of junk and jury-rigged equipment. How did I come to be here, in this maelstrom, alone in the vastness of Lake Michigan?

2

In the Beginning

In the spring of 1951 when I was almost 13 years old, Dad announced we were moving from Manistee to Ludington, Michigan to shorten his commute to work. He was the Superintendent of the Ludington & Northern Railway (L&N), also known to locals as "the sand train." Thousands of carloads of sand, destined mainly for factories casting automotive parts and even green glass Coke bottles, were dug from the giant sand dunes north of our new hometown.

We started our new lives on Lake Michigan's eastern shore in a very tiny house called Peek-A-Boo Cottage, one of only two cottages inhabited year-round in an iconic summer resort. It was every kid's dream of the perfect place to live. A few hundred feet from our front door, I could see Lincoln Lake, more than a mile long and about a third of a mile wide. This little lake offered fishing, turtle hunting, and even some "seaweed" swimming among the tadpoles and lily pads.

To the west, Lake Michigan with its spectacular beaches, lay only a few hundred yards away. In the carnival atmosphere of summer, something was always going on in that busy resort. It never occurred to me that not all people lived like this. However, during winter months, the Schrader kids next door (Nancy, Berry, Bobbie, and Jackie) were my only playmates. We entertained ourselves with ice skating, sledding, and snowball wars along the frozen shore. Western Michigan's famed deep snow and steep hills made for exciting rides on a steel-runner sled after arduous treks uphill.

Early in the winter of 1952, I ran across a plan in a youth magazine for a 14-foot wooden, flat-bottomed boat that could 'easily' be constructed by anyone. Enthralled with the idea of owning my very own rowboat, I decided to build it. When I proposed this project to my Dad, he quickly pointed out the pitfalls and expressed his skepticism of my grand plan. But I persisted. After all, we had a garage my father never used for his company truck or anything else because it sat, inconveniently, some 100 feet from our house. However, as my potential boat works, it had a few drawbacks: no heat, no electricity, and no daylight. Worse, I had only a few hand tools and no experience ever constructing anything of this size or complexity.

But Dad was game to let me try and agreed to buy one board or piece at a time as I needed it. He likely assumed I would lose interest and fizzle out quickly. Amazingly enough, over ensuing weeks that soon turned into months, I hand-sawed, screwed and glued together a wooden-sided, three-seat, plywood-bottomed scow. Early on, naysayers were numerous. Several adult friends and even a couple of resort workmen who observed my labors all declared it dead before completion: "that thing will never float well enough to carry anyone, and if it does, it'll leak so bad you'll sink." "Leak like a sieve" was the verdict, mainly because of the screwed-on plywood bottom. No one believed a 14-year-old kid working with no supervision could build a real boat.

As the days of winter wore on, I persevered for many evenings with cold hands and dim light, propelled by my dream of going out on Lincoln Lake in my homemade boat and fishing for the bass and northern pike I knew were there. Mom made sure I had warm drinks when I came in from the cold. Dad kept buying the raw boards, observing the construction and occasionally offered some advice, but he never took part in any physical labor. Slowly but surely, the boards and screws came together so it looked like a boat, more-or-less according to the magazine plans. For a high school freshman, it was a long, lonely and painful undertaking, making mistake after mistake. But in the process, I learned a few things about woodworking, frozen hands, and the power of persistence.

One day in April, when the ice had finally melted from the lake, I painted my new boat blue with some old surplus paint and mounted the oar locks. The Schrader kids and I carried the scow to the water's edge and held a launch ceremony. Lo and behold, not only did it float, it did not leak! I was ecstatic! My time in the cold and lonely garage was over. No more trying to read instructions by the dim illumination of a fading flashlight. To celebrate, I rowed around for a few minutes and imagined all the fun I'd be enjoying when spring became summer.

Dad made sure I didn't have to wait that long. Periodically, a repairman who serviced the two-way radio on L&N's new 1952 diesel electric locomotive would arrive in Ludington. Thompson was not only a radio technician but an avid fisherman. Next thing I knew, Dad arranged to have me take him fishing whenever he was in town. And this went on until I left for college. I was the rower and fishing guide; he was the bait caster looking for trophy fish while playing hooky from his job. One day, as we were busy casting off a patch of lily pads, a granddaddy northern pike hit my bait with such force it came completely out of the water in a whirling, twisting, line-breaking dance that ended with a spectacular, cannon-ball splash. I thought Thompson was going to jump right out of the boat trying to catch that monster with his bare hands. He was so excited, and the fish was so startling, I froze in mid crank reeling in the line—not the thing to do. Thompson blurted out, "Oh my god!" "Watch your line," "Holy cow," "Where's the net," "What the hell was that?" He sounded like an auctioneer on a caffeine overdose. By the time he got his blood pressure under control, the big fish had disappeared. Thompson immediately cast his line out where the water rings still rippled, but to no avail. The fish was gone. I was all bummed out because I had lost my favorite casting spoon. Thompson, on the other hand, was buzzed for months with the tale of 'the big one' that got away. Those memorable outings with Thompson and our man-to-boy conversations out on the lake influenced me in many ways I never realized until much later when I became an electronics technician and systems engineer.

Contrary to the dim forecasts of those early observers, my homemade boat never leaked. And the vivid memories of being in that little scow are as good as anyone could ever wish for. The experience taught me to ignore adversity and negativity and just go on about my business. Don't quit a dream simply because things go wrong or you make a mistake. Stick with it long enough and your diligence will pay a dividend.

Although my career choice (electrical engineering) may have been influenced by Thompson's mentoring, my lifelong hobby of amateur (ham) radio grew independently and matured in Ludington while attending high school. This avocation yielded many lifelong friends who stayed with me through good times and bad. In fact, I've never lost touch with my Ludington or Lansing connections or my passion for ham radio. Little did I know how important those folks would turn out to be, but they have added a wonderful dimension to my day-to-day adult life. After attending Michigan State University for four years where I met and married a girl, I pursued a career in electronics while we built a family of seven kids. Since I held both amateur and commercial radio and television licenses, these FCC documents allowed me to work in commercial broadcasting stations and two-way radio systems engineering and maintenance jobs.

By 1968, life with a houseful of kids in East Lansing was a blur of family responsibilities, a very busy communications industry job, and a nation in turmoil. Race riots, civil rights marches, and anti-war rallies dominated news headlines. Two prominent and popular American leaders (Martin Luther King Jr. and Robert Kennedy) were assassinated. And a controversial political campaign made Richard Nixon our next U.S. President. Coincidentally, with his inauguration in January 1969, I received the tragic news from my sister Gail that our mother had died unexpectedly of a stroke.

Immediately after my mother's death and funeral, I returned to East Lansing, packed up my five-year-old daughter Wendy and son, Kelly, who was three, and headed back to Ludington to stay with Dad for a week. He needed some family support during this stressful time to help him transition back into his old work routine at the Ludington and Northern Railway. A couple of kids running around would keep him occupied with good things to relieve his sadness.

However, this diversionary plan backfired on me when, on the third day in town, Dad had to drive me to the Ludington Hospital to have a ruptured appendix removed. For the next 12 days my surgeon, Dr. Rudolph Castellani, and the hospital staff had to put up with me while I recovered from the emergency operation and complications of a peritonitis infection. Months later when my ill-advised trip on Lake Michigan went sour, I was told on first-hand authority that Dr. Castellani's comment when he learned of my infamous rescue on Lake Michigan was: "We saved him for this?"

When my friends in Western Michigan's amateur radio community discovered I was in the hospital locally, they took it upon themselves to help me recover. Their visits renewed many old friendships with buddies from Ludington High School as well as friends in the ham radio network. As a result, my winter travails gave me a very supportive local fan base, and our family tragedy helped me develop a new frame of mind—one my Dad already practiced—for coping with an uncertain and often tumultuous future: "Don't buy green bananas." In other words, "Live life to the fullest today because no one knows what tomorrow will bring."

3

The Wager

Growing up on Michigan's western shore bounded by Lake Michigan made me an expert on the Great Lakes, or so I thought! After all, I had played winter and summer on the lake's beaches, climbed its incredible sand dunes, ducked through its waves, and defied its riptides and undertows. I was "lake smart." Had I not been so conceited about my self-declared knowledge, I probably could have avoided being ensnared in a bet as dangerous as any undertow. But I walked into the trap open-eyed with jaws a-flapping, like a beach tourist ignoring the red "DANGER" flag.

That life changing incident happened at my $200 a week job as a two-way radio systems technician for Troup Electronics in Jackson, Michigan. This electronics repair work introduced me to an interesting variety of places and people. We designed, installed, maintained and repaired radio communications systems for government, public safety, industrial and business enterprises many years before cellular telephone systems came into being. Every few days, and sometimes more often, I drove my red GMC service van 35 miles south to Jackson to visit the Troup home office to restock parts, turn in paperwork, and catch up on company gossip. Usually, I showed up at the service shop early wearing my uniform–dull grey shirt with a big Motorola emblem on the back. It was an unquestioned entry badge for anywhere we needed to go, including secret and secure places like maximum security jails, Oldsmobile's semi-secret experimental engineering garage, or the press box of Michigan State University's football stadium. I have stood within a few feet of Pat Nixon, wife of then U.S. President Richard Nixon, and ridden in fire and police vehicles speeding with full lights and sirens to emergency calls. All of this and more were considered normal on-the-job activities for a young telecommunications technician in the 1960s.

These fascinating encounters and experiences were the stories we shared with the other radio technicians at Troup Electronics before another busy day of service calls began. Sometimes our gang of six technicians and our boss, Fred Behnke, would drive the fleet of bright red company vans to our favorite coffee and donut shop, Kings Point Restaurant on M-60, for our gossip and stories swap meet.

On one particular spring day in early 1969 the topic of Lake Michigan came up. And I, as a veteran lake shore dweller and know-it-all, didn't hesitate to let everyone in earshot know I knew everything about the Great Lakes. And I made sure my boss Fred, a fellow loudmouth, knew of my superior knowledge. Fred, a 6'5" long-armed man, generally led, by dint of volume and dramatic gestures, all discussions and wild story-telling sessions. Fred had a talent for intimidating his victims while making them laugh uproariously at the same time. On that fateful morning, I became the target. We were discussing boats and the Great Lakes and in not-to-be-challenged tones, Fred opined it takes a pretty large boat to go across Lake Michigan or any of the Great Lakes. He, of course, was also an "expert" on this topic because he had grown up on the shores of Lake Huron.

"Baloney," I said. "You could cross Lake Michigan in any small boat."

The debate, as usual, was loud and involved everyone in the restaurant who cared to listen. We went up and down the verbal jousting road parrying questions with statements. What kind of boat would one take to go fishing as opposed to traveling from port to port? How big would the engine have to be? Could one go all the way across Lake Michigan with just a compass for navigation? Fred, with an evil smile and the growing sense of a verbal smack down in progress, looked me in the eye as if questioning a small child over who spilled the milk as it dawned on me I was being backed into a verbal corner. Everyone was agreeing with Fred that it takes a relatively large boat to navigate across or around the Great Lakes. As the boisterous discussion progressed, I eventually blurted out:

"Navigating on the Great Lakes is so simple that a raft of beer cans or even a bathtub, just like in the cartoons, could make it across Lake Michigan."

The guys all knew I really didn't know beans about boating or seamanship or anything else associated with Lake Michigan. Fred, for his part, was not exactly a dictionary of nautical knowledge either. But we didn't let a little ignorance get in the way of a good debate. So, the stage was set for the obvious. Fred stuck out his hand grinning, and with a wink to the entire restaurant, said:

"I'll bet you five bucks you can't float a beer can raft or a bathtub across Lake Michigan."

Considering that five dollars in those days was a good hourly wage for anybody, the proposed dollar amount was enough to put the sting of defeat in proper perspective. I could not resist the temptation of Fred's extended hand and the surreal encouragement of the eager onlookers. Besides, I didn't have time to contemplate just how ridiculous Fred's challenge sounded. It took me about one second to stick my hand out and give Fred a firm handshake. I was now bound by tradition and the honor of all radio technicians to either get on with a floating beer-can raft or a bathtub rig or pay up.

Fred figured on tormenting me for many moons over our nautical wager, and then getting five dollars to boot. Only a fool or a desperate bettor would ever think you could actually make either a raft of beer cans or a bathtub into a boat. But at that time, I had no idea of just how un-seaworthy a craft made of beer cans or a heavy cast iron bathtub really would be.

4

The Bathtub Craft is Born

Early on in this bizarre quest, I investigated the possibility of making a raft of beer cans and sailing it across Lake Michigan. Surely some beer company could make an attention-getting TV commercial of the man so anxious to drink their beer he floated across Lake Michigan to Milwaukee on a raft of empty beer cans. The problem with that idea?

I calculated it would take 5,000 empty cans to make a raft large enough to float myself, a motor, and fuel for a 60-mile trip. And it didn't take long to realize the beer cans would not only have to be empty but sealed, and they'd also have to be glued or otherwise fastened together to achieve a usable watercraft. Probably more important, I've never been much of a beer drinker. All of these obstacles finally convinced me the bathtub was the only way to prove Fred wrong and win the bet. Just like in the cartoons, you put an outboard motor on a bathtub, make sure the stopper is in and the shower works, and you can easily navigate the high seas.

The story of how an old cast-iron bathtub became a world-famous watercraft is just as implausible as my impulsive bet with Fred. As it turned out, destiny was hiding in plain sight. In other words, I was damn lucky a whole bunch of times.

First, I didn't build it. Second, all the major parts, including the tub, were donated, loaned or salvaged scrap materials. Most interesting of all, the final product—the bathtub raft itself—was built and outfitted by a diverse group of volunteers who donated their time, services, and materials simply because they wanted to be part of such an unusual venture. Of course, this all took place many, many years before YouTube, Facebook, Twitter, Snapchat, Google and the other social media that now shape our personal relationships. In 1969, my social circles were conducted face-to-face or by a wired telephone or a manually typed letter. In reflection, the bathtub craft's creation became a community effort of teasing, curiosity, humor, and genuine friendships.

No one, especially the Troup Electronics gang, thought I'd actually do anything about the bathtub bet; I certainly didn't. To be honest, I was hoping they'd all forget about the coffee klatch bragging and betting episode. And they might have, except that human nature and chance circumstances have a strange way of twisting fate.

Word of the bet somehow got out at the worksite of one of my clients. The Diamond Reo Corp. made a popular line of large trucks used by over-the-road freight haulers, wrecker services, and other industrial businesses. Roger Simmer, a parts chaser, worked at Diamond Reo's Lansing facility. His job was to drive a small truck—basically a motor driven, flatbed vehicle about the size of a golf cart—picking up and delivering items for the truck assembly operation. These parts trucks all had two-way radios so that a central dispatcher could send them off at breakneck speeds anywhere in the plant when a part was needed. Of course, either the two-way radios or the plant's radio paging system would occasionally fail and that's where I came in. I would drive into the plant in my little Troup Electronics service van and repair whatever electronic equipment was broken. When word got out that I had made a bet about some hair-brained scheme with a bathtub, my new persona as 'itinerant repairman-turned-nautical-stuntman' bore the brunt of unending crude jokes. I suspected Greg Hiscock, my fellow electronics technician, must have spilled the beans about the bathtub bet, but to this day he denies it.

One day, I was in the Diamond Reo plant when Roger Simmer heard me testing a radio and called on his two-way radio to ask if I would be interested in an old bathtub. Unfortunately, the entire truck plant heard that call. For days afterward, whenever I visited the plant, someone would ask about the health and welfare of Roger's bathtub. I would then explain that I didn't really have Roger's bathtub, and my threat of a boating trip in a bathtub was just a big joke. Finally, however, to stop the razzing, I decided to call Roger's bluff and tell everyone I was serious about the bet. The next day I told Roger I was ready for the bathtub.

The next evening, he pulled into my driveway in East Lansing with an old, but very recognizable, Kohler cast-iron bathtub in his pickup truck. The classic curved feet were gone, but the holes for the drain and the water faucets were in their proper places. He said he was remodeling his house and figured it was easier to give it to me than throw it away. To this day, I still wonder if the guys at Diamond Reo, including Roger, didn't buy an old bathtub just to see what I would do with it.

That bathtub was the beginning of a long list of contributions to the bizarre bathtub venture over the next few weeks. Everyone, including me, assumed that it was an ongoing joke. It was great entertainment to be part of something so wildly outlandish. Besides, it got Fred Behnke's attention and made him think I was really planning to collect on our bet. Fred let me know he was most interested in my new driveway decoration. On my next trip to the service shop in Jackson, Fred suggested it would be quite entertaining for my neighbors if I would take a bath in the tub as it sat in my driveway. At our coffee klatch that morning, his animated acting of this bathing scenario was a true masterpiece of stand-up comedy. Fred colorfully described how I would be stark-naked standing in the bathtub with all the neighbors watching when the police arrived to haul me away as a nut case. And I, of course, would be screaming and throwing water at the spectators as they cuffed me.

Within days, even my ham radio friends learned of my weird bet with my boss. The now notorious bathtub was sitting in my driveway when a friend, Earl "Ed" Grable stopped by for some help fixing his ham radio. Ed and his brothers ran a metal machine shop in Dimondale, southwest of Lansing. When Ed saw the forlorn bathtub sitting there, he wanted to know what in the world I was doing with it. By the time I finished my story of the wager, he had completely forgotten his original mission. Ed offered so many suggestions on how to make the thing float that I suggested he take charge of the project. Amazingly, within a few minutes, he was busy planning the tub-to-boat conversion!

No one could have imagined just how difficult this undertaking was going to be. First, the cast-iron bathtub weighed at least 200 pounds. In fact, as a flotation device, it weighed so much it couldn't float even if completely empty. It displaced less weight of water than it weighed. In other words, the old tub would sink like a rock if launched into water. But this perplexing problem didn't deter Ed in the least. The obvious solution, Ed said, was to fasten some empty metal barrels to it for flotation so it wouldn't sink. That sounded easy enough at first. However, a heavy, cast iron bathtub does not lend itself well to having anything fastened to it that might survive waves and heavy seas. Nevertheless, Ed dispatched me to a local salvage company where I found four, empty, 30-gallon barrels which I proudly trucked home. Unfortunately, Ed thought I would buy the more standard 55-gallon drums. When he eyed the barrels, his first reaction was that they just wouldn't displace enough water. After some calculations, however, he decided the smaller barrels might just barely work.

Oh well, I thought, what's a few pounds of flotation more-or-less. Although Ed expressed grave concerns about my intelligence as well as my sanity, next thing I knew he had designed a problem-solving rig. He built an angle iron frame and threaded solid steel rods to hold the barrels to the tub in what was loosely referred to as a 'raft' configuration. Suddenly, the joke project took on new, more serious dimensions. The real possibility of a floatable bathtub now sat in my driveway, and I had acquired a crew of co-conspirators to further my cause.

When Fred Behnke learned about the new bathtub raft, he expressed surprise I would go to so much bother for such a useless bet. He also began to worry publicly among our work group that I had gone off the deep end of mental health. From my viewpoint, I certainly enjoyed seeing Fred worrying that maybe, just maybe, I was serious about our public wager. And I was.

As the bathtub project slowly took shape from a growing pile of metal parts in my driveway, I envisioned some miracle letting me paddle my way to a five-dollar victory over Fred. It was not beyond possible that a successful trip across the Grand River in Lansing would be enough to convince Fred to call our bet a draw. You can imagine the conversations that ensued whenever I made my regular visits to Troup headquarters. Fred was enjoying the tormenting and teasing more every day. Among my co-workers, the bathtub in my driveway kept the gossip stove hot. Jokes flew and barbs were traded. Fred seemed confident I would stop the nonsense when I came to my senses. I, of course, hoped for a miracle that would save me from having to admit this project was going down the drain.

5

Testing the Bathtub Project: Will It Float?

My list of win-the-bet boosters grew daily. It wasn't that they thought the bathtub would actually float; they just wanted to be in on the fun. Take Lt. Don Hewson of the East Lansing Police Department: he was my contact when ELPD's radio equipment needed service. But he knew Ed Grable through a small side business they owned reloading pistol ammunition, and both were ham radio buffs. We three spent many evenings together talking ham radio. Early on, when Ed told him about my bathtub project, Don offered to transport the soon-to-be watercraft in his pickup truck.

The bathtub and loose barrels soon made their first trip to Ed's place in Dimondale to be assembled. The newly created vessel consisted of the stark white bathtub with rounded edges, surrounded by four metal barrels all held together by two-inch angle iron. Threaded, solid steel rods created the compression fit to secure the tub between the barrels.

Thanks to Ed's ingenuity, the rig was very sturdy. He figured if I was crazy enough to take this thing into a river or out on a lake then it certainly wasn't going to sink or break apart. No one said it had to look pretty, either. In fact, the old tub craft looked as ugly as a raft of barrels could look. Even in our wildest dreams, neither Ed nor I ever imagined his durable design would one day get tested to its structural limits.

Now back in my driveway, the 'bathtub thing,' as my kids called it, had grown into a vessel we hoped would float. And after Greg Hiscock got involved, we grew more confident it would. Greg was a young electronics technician fresh out of college who also worked for Troup. He was there at Kings Point Restaurant when I made the bet with Fred, and had a keen interest in my quest to win it. He suggested I bring the bathtub raft out to his family's farm so he could seal up the tub's open drain hole. He'd use his Dad's welding equipment.

Once again, Hewson's pickup transported the now heavier rig to the farm for its next improvement.

To my surprise, when I stopped by to inspect the welding job, I spied some unsolicited "artwork." Greg had very carefully used melted welding rod to create the words "Vic's Folly" on the rear angle iron for all to see.

I was a little peeved at first. I thought the raft deserved a grander more nautical name, like "Lake Michigan Queen." But I couldn't erase welding. Thanks to Greg, the bathtub raft now had a name befitting its owner.

My growing gang of co-conspirators was equally bent on my winning the five-dollar bet with Fred Behnke. These neophyte marine engineers wanted to see the bathtub-barrel raft in the water. Would it float? Bets on both sides of the question flew back and forth. But we felt ready for the test. Into Don's truck it went again. To avoid curious eyes, we hauled it to the Grand

River near Grand Ledge, west of Lansing.The big question for today was: Would this conglomeration of junk parts and bent iron float well enough for someone to ride in it?

Photo by Vic Jackson
This photo was taken in June 1969 with the Jackson kids
and the assembled bathtub "raft". Left to right: Gene age 2,
Victor "Lee" age 8, Wendy age 4, Robin age 1, Kelly age 3,
Kevin age 7

Remarkably, it did. The flotation test on the Grand River was a major step in the conversion of the bathtub into a watercraft.

However, even without an occupant, the rig displaced so much water it looked like it wanted to sink rather than float. It was very ungainly to paddle and quite inefficient as a canoe. Lack of a keel and a very low freeboard all around created a very real, practical problem as well. Would even a small wave wash me out of the tub.

Photo by Greg Hiscock

Propulsion was the obvious solution. If I couldn't paddle or row this thing across a river, I'd never make it across 60 miles of Lake Michigan. Forget transforming it into a sailboat; there was no room for a mast, and I didn't know anything about sailing. A motor was deemed the single most important addition. However, with a motor I would have to carry fuel. Both additions increased the craft's weight. It also dawned on me that if I was going to navigate out of sight of land I needed some navigation gear, like a compass. Which then presented another problem: where in the world do you mount a magnetic compass on a cast iron bathtub? A magnetic compass points to north because the compass needle is a magnet attracted to the magnetic field of the earth. The challenge when mounting a

23

compass on a cast-iron bathtub is to install it so the compass needle will point to north instead of to the bathtub.

Greg took a picture of that first launch showing me standing knee deep in water inside the floating bathtub, my pants legs barely rolled up high enough to stay dry and a bailing can in my hand. The picture suggests I was bailing water out for dear life to stay afloat, but I was bailing water into the tub to test how much it would hold before sinking.

Photo by Greg Hiscock

The water torture test on the Grand River was judged a success, but it pointed out the many problems we still needed to overcome before attempting any real travel on water. However, the tub had floated and could, therefore, be called a watercraft. Now I had something to hold over Fred. Maybe he would concede and just cancel our bet. Unfortunately for me, I never got a chance to confront Fred or negotiate cancellation of our wager. Fate stepped in and swept me along with it.

6

A Fateful Meeting with the Mayor

Amateur Radio operators have provided communications services in times of disaster and for all kinds of public service activities almost since radio communications have existed. When the chips are down and all other means of communication fail, ham radio operators use their own radio gear and sometimes risk their lives to maintain communications in the public interest.

Annually, hundreds of amateur (ham) radio clubs and individual amateur radio operators around the USA, and in other countries, test their communication skills under simulated disaster circumstances in an exercise called Field Day.

On Sunday, June 29, 1969, I attended the Central Michigan Amateur Radio Club's Field Day at Camp Kiwanis near Mason, Michigan. The club set up several high frequency two-way radio communications facilities and were busy making contacts with other stations' Field Day stations around the country.

Gerald Graves, in his official capacity as the Mayor of the City of Lansing, visited field day activities to inspect the City of Lansing's Emergency Services vehicle at the scene. Mayor Graves was being introduced to the ham operators crowded around a busy transmitter-receiver when someone jokingly mentioned that one of the local radio operators present was planning a little trip in his bathtub across Lake Michigan. Subsequently, I was introduced to His Honor the Mayor by Jim Holcomb, Director of Lansing's Emergency Services Operations, as the would-be bathtub sailor. Then someone suggested His Honor might like to take a ride with me in the tub. A roar of laughter erupted.

It was merely a twist of fate that both he and I were present when that tongue-in-cheek idea was voiced. Little did I know that Mayor Gerry Graves was a 1944 graduate of the US Merchant Marine Academy and a former ship's captain. Apparently, this unusual nautical connection was too much of a coincidence for him to let pass. Mayor Graves requested that I come to his Lansing office the following Monday morning during his weekly press conference and repeat my offer of a ride. After all, a little publicity wouldn't hurt his political career. Besides, in those troubling times, everyone knew the press corps covering city hall needed a good laugh.

No one could have imagined my next few days.

7

Publicity and the Local News

As requested, I appeared in City Hall at 10 a.m. Monday morning, June 30. The Mayor's assistant asked me to wait in a small office for a few minutes while the press conference got underway. A few minutes later, Mayor Graves called me in and introduced me to the press corps (all two of them). The mayor wanted them to hear more about my offer of a ride, and the newsmen light heartedly asked us both some 'serious' questions:

Did I work for the Mayor's political opposition? Maybe I would take him for a one-way ride? Which of us was going to paddle? Who was going to command the vessel? Had His Honor checked with city council for permission to go? Would this excursion be at city expense? Would we be going with or without clothes?

Obviously dazzled by the media's attention, but realizing the potential hazards of the venture, Mayor Graves decided to decline my offer while the press was present. The reporters loved it. The offer of a ride, that is. But they were skeptical. Maybe it was junk news! They wanted to see this purported bathtub craft and take some pictures. After all, what if the Mayor was trying to pull a fast one on them? Maybe these ham radio nuts just cooked the whole thing up. And they were not entirely wrong. To prove he had not gone completely bonkers, His Honor agreed to visit East Lansing and inspect the bathtub craft himself. Besides, he too was a little dubious about my story and wanted to see the notorious nautical marvel with his own eyes.

On schedule, later that afternoon Mayor Graves, along with a couple of curious aides, a Lansing State Journal reporter and a photographer, arrived at my little red Ann Street house to check out the lonely bathtub craft sitting in the driveway.

A festive mood prevailed as the Mayor looked things over very carefully under the watchful eyes of the news team and decided his initial reaction was correct. The bathtub really wasn't big enough for the two of us, and he would sit this one out on shore. They asked me to sit in the bathtub and pose for pictures. Reporter Dave Hanson subsequently filed a story to the Lansing State Journal and to the wire services describing how the Mayor of Lansing, a former Merchant Marine skipper, had turned down my offer of a ride in a bathtub across Lake Michigan. We all agreed the local folks would get a laugh or two out of this story.

That afternoon, the Journal published a story designed to get the attention of His Honor's political enemies.

Newspaper headline: "Graves Refuses Ride"
"Rub a Dub Dub: Man to Cross Lake Michigan in Tub"
Lansing State Journal
July 1, 1969, Lansing, Michigan

29

The bathtub bet had now gone public!

At 6 a.m. the next morning, my telephone rang. Picking up the handset, I answered the old desk-type phone beside my bed. Still not fully awake, I didn't understand what was being said at first. It was someone speaking very fast, in a loud voice saying something about this is KXXX or whatever, and would I tell the audience about the bathtub. Here I am in bed, roused out of a sound sleep, and suddenly I'm talking live on radio to some unknown audience somewhere. I was somewhat puzzled by all of the fervent questions because I couldn't remember clearly what I had told the newspaper reporter the previous day. The questions were asked half in jest and half seriously. Was I really, really going to go out on Lake Michigan in that bathtub? Was the shower head still working? What would I do if the bathtub sank? I finally managed to get through that interview and set the phone down.

It immediately rang again. More ranting and raving from somewhere far away and more of the same off-the-wall questions. It was as if radio interviewers from hell were tormenting me in a dream. As soon as I would put the phone down it would ring again. I would answer and it would be another interview. The media frenzy was mind boggling. How in the world did these people know anything about my bathtub? Finally, it dawned on me: somehow that story of the Mayor and my offer of a bathtub ride had been transmitted by news wire to the entire country and beyond. The telephone calls continued for the next hour or so, until I finally wised up and took the phone off the hook. I realized I had become famous, but I didn't quite understand what the uproar was all about. What I did understand after this episode was why famous people have unlisted and unpublished telephone numbers.

By this time, my kids also began to realize that I had achieved some sort of notoriety. We caught our three-year-old son Kelly leaving the house with one of my shoes. He figured if I was famous, my shoes would be bigger than his friend's Dad's shoes. They were meeting midway to prove whose theory was right. Never mind the physical logic, I was probably a foot shorter than the neighbor.

On Tuesday afternoon, July 1, 1969, the Lansing State Journal published a photo of me sitting in my bathtub "barge." A large coil of rope hangs over the front of the bathtub. Perched on one of the barrels is some kind of electronic equipment. I am sitting in the back of the bathtub supposedly reading a map. If ever there was a picture taken to prove someone was a real kook, this one ranks right up there near the top.

The publicity was beginning to be a burden on my everyday life. Everywhere I went, someone stopped me to ask about my proposed bathtub trip across Lake Michigan. I was having trouble getting my work done. Although it was exciting to be so popular, I wasn't sure I could survive the fame. Everyone I met also thought it was a big joke. And no one, including me, thought I would ever actually attempt such a foolhardy venture. My efforts to pull a joke on Fred had rapidly turned into a serious challenge for me. How I was going to weasel out of this dilemma?

Almost everyone at some time in their life yearns to be famous—a sports hero, or a movie star. The glamour and prominence associated with being a "somebody" sounds exciting. Even strangers know your name. Now a 'nobody' like me had suddenly achieved that goal. The difficulty with this status is that you are never alone, in public or sometimes even in private. You are constantly under surveillance as if you had a detective following your every move. Suddenly, privacy becomes a valuable commodity. I learned that one must be especially careful when talking to anyone except close friends. Your joking comment or a misunderstood statement might appear in headlines the next day. I also learned that the public associates fame with wealth, that somehow popularity generates money. True for movie stars, but for the rest of us the paychecks stay the same regardless of the headlines. And I still had to find the time to get my work done.

8

Help from Many Quarters

The publicity was generating offers of help and encouragement. Everyone wanted to see me actually get in the tub and go somewhere. Reporters called regularly to check on my plans. I think they were hoping the Mayor might change his mind.

One of the most generous offers of assistance came from a client, Richard "Dick" Cahill. He owned an answering service and radio paging company in Lansing. In fact, Cahill Answering Service handled the Troup Electronics service line in the Lansing area. Dick was one of many of my service accounts that had taken a keen interest in my bathtub bet after reading about it in the newspaper. One day, while fixing his radio pagers (beepers), I mentioned that I was having problems hauling my bathtub craft around, because it was now so heavy. Lifting the rig up and down into Don Hewson's truck was back breaking work. Dick, formerly a General Motors industrial engineer knew how to solve engineering problems. He suggested his snowmobile trailer would be the ideal vehicle for hauling around a heavy, ungainly bathtub boat. The trailer tilted down for loading, it could be backed into the water for launching, it was easy to pull behind a car and it was free. The "free" part got my attention. From that moment on, Dick's snowmobile trailer served me well for transporting the bathtub rig around Michigan. I used it into the next winter while his own snowmobiles rusted away on the ground. The ability to easily haul my heavy bathtub rig around without help was a vast improvement over the armstrong method needed with a pickup truck.

About this time, I received another generous offer from Gordon and Polly Forgar, owners of Forgars Boat City of Lansing. Having read the newspaper article about my planned trip, they too wanted to support the venture. The Forgars said they had an outboard motor that looked like an ideal candidate for powering the newly created bathtub craft. It was a 20 horsepower Chrysler with electric start, a generator to charge the battery, and a plug-in fuel fitting. Gasoline cans with suitably equipped hoses could be plugged into the engine quickly and easily, thus allowing multiple cans to be carried in the craft. The Forgars and I signed the outboard lease agreement for one dollar. We painted "Forgars Boat City of Lansing" on both sides of the engine's top cowling as pay back for their generosity.

Now that the tub was a powered boat, I needed to register it with the State of Michigan as a watercraft so the Coast Guard or some other government agency would have no excuse to keep my bathtub rig on shore. I was a bit apprehensive about what might happen in the registration attempt, but the process went without a hitch. I filled out the papers indicating that my homebuilt watercraft was five feet long, made of cast iron and steel, and had a capacity of one person. When I casually mentioned to the clerk in the Michigan Secretary of State's office that it was a bathtub, her eyebrows rose—she obviously thought I was just joking—and she continued shuffling the paperwork. So, with little fanfare, she approved my application, assigned my watercraft identification numbers, and gave me an official watercraft registration. My contraption now had the State's permission to be a motorboat, and I could legally ride the waters of the State and the Great Lakes.

Photo by Vic Jackson

The projected trip was now serious business for me. I had the tail of a wild tiger in my hands and I couldn't let go. My boss, Fred Behnke, would be happy; I had run out of excuses not to honor our bet.

9

Making a Bathtub into a Watercraft

During my investigation of how to ride this bathtub watercraft across Lake Michigan, some unusual issues surfaced: How would I sit in the contraption when underway? How would I keep important stuff dry, such as maps or gear? Would the barrels collapse when pounded by heavy waves? How much buoyancy did the barrels have? What if they leaked?

The next big challenge was how and where to mount the comparatively heavy outboard motor? The answer was a wooden board mounted across the rear as a transom. Next came some very large washers combined with a wooden back-plate, which sealed up the tub's obvious big leaks where faucets had been.

Once the outboard was mounted, we started running tests of the elemental bathtub watercraft. Lee Gillette, a business acquaintance, allowed me to use his private lake near East Lansing for more water testing. I had trouble doing any testing in public places because a curious crowd would immediately gather to gawk and get in the way whenever I appeared with the bathtub rig in tow.

We quickly determined that I needed something to protect me from waves more than a foot high. Without protection, water would wash over the front of the tub with considerable force whenever I encountered even mildly choppy water, or if I slowed down too quickly. This very significant problem had to be solved or the bathtub could never be used on Lake Michigan where one-foot waves are considered smooth water.

Once again, we asked Ed Grable, our unpaid resident designer and construction chief, for ideas. Within a short time, Ed did a magnificent job of freehand metal artistry with some 20-gauge sheet steel. Cutting, bending, forming and welding the metal around the bathtub, he created a splash shield across the front and sides of the tub. It was the perfect answer to a knotty problem, but definitely not cosmetic. Comical might be a better description because it looked as if a mangled umbrella was stuck to the front. My so-called watercraft was now a very strange looking vessel, indeed.

There were two, thirty-gallon barrels on each side of the bathtub. These barrels were welded end to end. A piece of two-inch angle iron was bent around the top and sides of the barrel ends and across the top rim of the bathtub. The angle irons were held in compression by four, one-inch diameter round steel rods threaded on each end. Large nuts and lock washers were tightened down on the steel rods to hold barrels and tub together in a tight grip.

To streamline the water flow, 20-gauge sheet-steel cones were welded on the front of the barrels. However, the nose cones proved to be perfectly useless when underway because they protruded out and above the water line. But they definitely added to the bizarre appearance of "Vic's Folly."

Photo by Paul Zarkovich

Meanwhile, design work and calculations continued because we still had a lot of unanswered questions about the craft's seaworthiness in the real world of waves and wind. As my Dad had said on numerous occasions, I was an "ignoramus" when it came to nautical knowledge, navigation, and a few other subjects as well.

However, some logistical decisions had to be made now. What route would I take across this awesome, 307-mile-long lake? Where would I launch from? What was the best destination? How much fuel would I need? How and where would I carry it?

I calculated that the 20-horsepower outboard motor would consume about two gallons of gasoline per hour. I also decided to cross the lake from Ludington, Michigan to Manitowoc, Wisconsin, a distance of approximately 60 miles. At a rate of six miles per hour, the trip would take about 10 hours. By adding a reserve of five more hours of fuel "just in case," meant I would need 30 gallons of gasoline. So, I'd somehow have to transport five, six-gallon cans.

Needless to say, the challenge was where to put 30 gallons of gasoline, given the space I needed for myself and other necessities: a full-size car battery, maps, shoes, dry socks, a camera, and a few odds and ends. This paraphernalia had to stay dry and secure in the tub when navigating big waves. My informal group of advisors, including Ed Grable, Don Hewson, and Greg Hiscock, debated how and where to stow my fuel supply. Finally, we decided I would tow a small raft for the gasoline, a plan that went untested in water. Later, when the waves on Lake Michigan were high and the water rough, I would severely regret this lack of preparation and testing.

Lack of a keel on this unseaworthy craft created a real navigation issue. How would I control the tub's direction in the wind and waves? We decided I would use the outboard motor to steer the craft, in effect creating a powered rudder. As a matter of necessity, I taped a stick to the outboard's throttle (steering arm) to extend it toward the front where I would be seated in a semi-reclining position. I could then grasp the stick without leaning back toward the rear, thereby keeping the transom and outboard motor from sinking under water. The rig, when moving through the water, floated nose-high at about a

20-degree angle, with the front end out of the water and the rear end dangerously close to flooding. The 'ole tub,' when underway, waddled like a dancing hippo. Precise weight distribution would be critical to staying afloat and alive.

Finally, we painted the splash shield white and the barrels day-glow orange. Ostensibly, this color combination made the bathtub craft more conspicuous to other boats, but it also created good visibility for potential rescuers. In order to stay comfortable, I bought a foam pad normally used under a sleeping bag. Folded, this pad provided some comfort from the hard bottom of the tub. However, when underway, the pad was always wet, so comfort was a matter of degree.

10

Ignorance is Bliss: Preparing for the Voyage

A trip across Lake Michigan generally requires some communications capability, some navigation skill and equipment, some planning of logistics, and more than a passing knowledge of weather. This is neat stuff to know but, unfortunately, I chose to learn as I went along. It was an expensive and embarrassing education that almost cost me my life.

Being an amateur radio operator, call sign W8BLP, I decided to use amateur (ham) radio for my communications. The problem is that almost all watercraft normally use public, well known marine frequencies and facilities. Therefore, I wouldn't be able to talk directly to the Coast Guard or other boats, but I could talk to a lot of other ham radio operators. If I needed to talk to other boats or the Coast Guard, the messages would have to be relayed first through the ham radio contacts on shore and then by wired telephone lines to a shore radio station that could communicate with the other vessel. This roundabout communications system was not very well understood by the Coast Guard, the news media, or the public and was, at best, inefficient for my needs; but it was the only practical solution to a vexing problem.

The big date for my lake crossing was set for July 5, 1969. I calculated that the day after the holiday would be ideal. The sun would be out, the beaches would be warm, and the big lake would be quite smooth. Unfortunately, the volume of my ignorance of weather and weather forecasting was only slightly bigger than my overwhelming ignorance of seamanship.

Headquarters for the bathtub trip was to be my Dad's little white house on the corner of Ludington and Gaylord Avenues in Ludington. I chose the Ludington, Michigan to Manitowoc, Wisconsin crossing for several reasons. First, having lived there, graduated from Ludington High School, and having my father still there, made it familiar territory. Second, I had a number of amateur radio operator friends who lived in or near Ludington along the lake. These hams offered to provide vital communications for the trip. Third, at that time, a ready means of transportation existed to cross the lake and return to Ludington via the Chesapeake and Ohio Railway Carferries* bound for Manitowoc, Milwaukee and Kewaunee, Wisconsin. The fourth and biggest reason for choosing this route was that it crossed the very heart of Lake Michigan. No one could ever accuse me of taking the easy way over or using a cheater's loophole to win the bet.

---

* The word "carferry," as used in this narration, refers to a ferry that was constructed to primarily transport railroad cars across bodies of water.

11

Media-Hyped Trip Begins

Early Friday morning, while the rest of the country prepared to celebrate the July 4th holiday, I finished readying the bathtub craft for its trip to Ludington and my anticipated voyage across Lake Michigan the next day. I could take advantage of this weekend holiday without missing any work.

The weather was mostly sunny, but typical of Michigan it could change at any moment. Weather, however, was not a major concern. I assumed that, outside of hitting a major storm, I'd make it across the lake just fine. I was prepared for waves a couple of feet high without any appreciable breaking surf, what Michigan natives call whitecaps. From shore and a landlubber's perspective, Lake Michigan waves normally look quite picturesque and non-threatening.

My one major concern that afternoon as I drove to Ludington towing the snowmobile trailer and my rig was the media I expected to find waiting for me. I anxiously planned how to handle the TV and newspaper reporters I knew would be there for the big launch. The whole family, including all the kids, were packed up for their festive holiday in my hometown. Friends, including my entire inner circle of helpers, eagerly anticipated my trip as the final chapter in the Vic Jackson-versus-Fred Behnke saga.

I arrived to a whirlwind of interviews, conversations with ham radio friends, and last minute preparations for the next day's water adventure. The festive atmosphere only added to my cavalier attitude and confidence in winning the great bathtub bet. My six children, however, were only mildly interested in the melodrama around them. The comings and goings of their father were normal every-day events. The occasional trip here or there with the strange bathtub-on-trailer thing was forgotten as they attended to the real fun activities with neighborhood kids.

To my way of thinking, problems with navigation or communications during the proposed bathtub trip seemed quite unlikely. The simple systems my advisory crew and I had devised seemed adequate and quite appropriate for this oddball venture. In retrospect, my bathtub craft was constructed and equipped exactly as you'd expect from someone unfamiliar with good seamanship or shipbuilding. Perhaps that's why both the news media and public had so much interest. The craft itself looked outlandish, and the whole idea of sailing in it struck people as funny. My totally unconventional, experimental marine systems included use of ham radio communications, a complete lack of reliable and redundant navigation gear, a single outboard motor using an untested fueling method and, most importantly, total ignorance of weather and weather forecasting for navigating on the Great Lakes.

In many ways, my ignorance was a blessing. I had no preconceived notions of how to do these things. Experienced boaters and yachtsmen alike who observed my preparations and so-called watercraft all exhibited a haughty attitude toward me. In truth, when most of these people went boating they never ventured out of sight of land in their vessels. Among my inner circle, the standing joke was to call them "Captain Tunas" because, obviously, they were "Chicken of the Sea", as is advertised by the canned tuna of the same name. As the summer progressed, however, my attitude toward the experienced boaters' fear of Great Lakes' waters would significantly change. Cruising out into a vast expanse of constantly changing water and weather conditions required more understanding and seamanship than I possessed.

My father was not at all impressed with my preparations and plans. Dad was also not very confident that I had any idea of where I was going or what I was doing! He found the whole operation extremely risky. In a last-ditch effort to dissuade me, he proposed an option that might satisfy the media: I could just motor around the harbor or make a short trip out into Lake Michigan, but under no circumstances should I attempt to venture beyond sight of land. Dad really didn't know anything about navigation either. His idea of a trip that would get me across Lake Michigan would be to follow a carferry across the lake. Because they always made it to Wisconsin and back, they obviously knew where they were going. It was a grand idea, but unrealistic; I couldn't keep up with a carferry going 18 miles an hour when my vessel could only go six miles an hour, at best. Well, he then suggested, perhaps the carferry would tow me across the lake. Somehow, I didn't think that idea would fly either. Can you imagine the conversation between the carferry captain and the Coast Guard trying to arrange such a stunt? The

Chesapeake and Ohio Railway Carferry company certainly would have been able to sell lots of tickets for the trip.

Ever desperate to keep me from embarking on a foolhardy trip, Dad then dreamed up the most novel way for me to win the bet without getting wet: just load the bathtub on the back of a ferry and ride across Lake Michigan sitting in the tub. That idea probably would have made the Coast Guard the happiest and the ferry company the most ticket revenue. But I would have been cheating on the bet. Besides, by now I truly believed taking the tub across the lake was going to be an easy and fun task.

That evening, to cover all my bases, I visited the Ludington Coast Guard station with my famous bathtub in tow. It was a courtesy visit so the men of U.S. Coast Guard Station Ludington could see the rig for themselves and agree with me that it was a seaworthy craft. They were surprisingly supportive but understandably skeptical. Translated, this means they had a good laugh and wished me luck. In a bit of fortuitous fortune telling, they also informed me I should call them if the bathtub sprang a leak or the shower quit working. I went to bed that evening with great anticipation of a routine but interesting trip that would put doubters and naysayers out of business. If nothing else, this notoriety was a pleasant diversion from my normal life. Tomorrow would be a grand and exciting day.

12

Reality and a Wild Ride

Before dawn that morning I called the Coast Guard for a weather report. I assumed they would know all about the weather on Lake Michigan since they were both U.S. Government agencies and instrumental in maintaining Great Lakes marine operations. The seaman who answered my call sounded quite professional as he read me the U.S. Weather Bureau's (Kansas City Weather Center) forecast for Lake Michigan for Saturday, July 5, 1969.

Happily, the forecast called for clear to scattered clouds, northwest winds 10 to 20 knots (12-23 miles per hour), with no more than two-foot swells for the entire day across the middle of the lake. If you are not out on the lake in a small boat, this sounds like a pretty good boating day. Belatedly, I learned that even 30-foot charter fishing boats on Lake Michigan stock barf bags for such surf.

When I stepped outside that morning, I confronted something totally unexpected: Fog. Thick fog. Really thick, wet, pea soup fog. The weather people failed to mention fog. No matter, I thought to myself, the day would certainly improve. The morning sun and predicted light winds would clear it off. The good news is that fog does go away when the wind picks up. That fact is also the bad news. As the wind accelerates, it whips up waves. And on this particular day, the wind decided to make big waves.

Meanwhile, Dad and my wife Ariel had worked out a grand plan for supporting my efforts. They would take the 7 a.m. carferry out of Ludington across the lake to Manitowoc, my destination. At the suggestion of a news reporter, they planned the trip in anticipation of waiting in Manitowoc to witness my grand arrival and a booming celebration. My sister, Gail, would care for the Jackson kiddie gang while the parents were occupied with a Lake Michigan trip. And if conditions were right, Ariel and Dad might even catch sight of me on their crossing from the ferry. It was a naive plan; although I did catch sight of the ferry as it departed Ludington harbor, it was too far away for anyone on the ship to see me bobbing up and down in the growing surf.

Before 5:30 a.m., I was off to the public boat launching ramp on Pere Marquette Lake with the bathtub rig in tow. This fairly large lake on the south side of Ludington forms the harbor for the carferry docks. By launching from this protected boat ramp on a calm inland lake, I would be able to get underway and test things a bit before heading out into the big lake. First things first: I checked the fuel cans to make sure they were full and untied the craft from the trailer. Then I readied the homemade raft holding the extra fuel. More than a few onlookers, reporters and well-wishers crowded around for this highly publicized effort. Some helped while I backed the trailer partially into the water to launch "Vic's Folly." Next went the raft holding the extra fuel. My high school buddy, Willard Lake from Ludington, was on hand to drive my car and empty trailer back to Dad's house. A holiday atmosphere buoyed our spirits on this summery Saturday, and the news media positioned themselves for the best possible photos of the bizarre "bathtub mariner" saga unfolding in south Ludington.

In retrospect, what really amazes me is how naive I was about my very dangerous undertaking. Here I was, about to get into a tiny untested craft, cruise out of the harbor in fog with less than 30 feet of visibility, and go merrily into Lake Michigan without the slightest clue that navigation or weather might be a problem for the next 60 miles of very deep, open water. To be honest, even though I had grown up in western Michigan, I lacked any real knowledge of the big lake. My lack of nautical experience should have been a big red flag. But ignorance is bliss. I was unaware of any impediments that could spoil a fine trip across the lake. After getting everything in order, I donned the life vest loaned to me by my brother-in-law, Art Breece, stowed my shoes and socks in the plastic trash can and turned the key to start the outboard motor. The fateful trip began.

As I pulled away from the launch ramp, I twisted my body around to see where I was going. Ordinarily, I would be facing aft toward the motor. But the thick fog prevented me from using the side-mounted mirror I had installed to see ahead. This contorted riding position made a rather odd sight, captured by a United Press International photographer, as I headed out on my cross-lake journey.

Newspapers across the country featured that photo the next day. It showed my strange watercraft with its trailing raft of gas cans and a U.S. flag flying atop my radio antenna while I steered sitting 'side-saddle' through what looked like high seas.

United Press International Photo

The truth is I was only 20 feet from the dock and still in the harbor struggling to get my vessel to track a straight course. The keel-less fuel raft was pulling my bathtub craft back and forth in a yawing motion. Fortunately, within a few seconds, onlookers lost sight of me and my struggle in the thick fog. I was only detectable to those on shore by the steady hum of the motor as I carefully made my way through Ludington harbor in the eerie quiet.

The advance of daylight produced only a faint lightening of the heavy mist. Passing carefully by the ghostly carferries in their slips, I followed the deep-water channel between the rock and concrete breakwaters into Lake Michigan. If all went well, my next stop would be Manitowoc, Wisconsin, 60 miles west. At six miles per hour, it would be an all-day journey. I could now feel a light breeze starting to blow out of the northwest. Out beyond the protective breakwaters, the deeper waters turned an ominous dark green, and the gentle wave swells stretched out and expanded into ocean-sized hills in a never-ending march. As minutes ticked by, the clearing sky revealed more worrisome signs. Under a now biting wind, the big lake's cold, deep water churned and spit up white, foam-topped waves.

Because of the publicity surrounding my early morning launch, the ferry crews had taken a keen interest in my proposed voyage and picked up my vessel on their radar as I made my way down the channel to the lake. Later, a carferry captain on one of the docked ships reported watching me leave the harbor. He said he lost me when I was just a short distance outside the breakwater because my craft was so small. He was definitely impressed, he said, by the bravery of the tiny tub's skipper going out on Lake Michigan in such awful weather conditions. In other words, he was amazed at my stupidity.

Crossing Lake Michigan in a Bathtub

My morning was not going well. Now several miles offshore, in a relentless string of pounding waves, my puny orange and white craft was trying to buck its way westward. Truly it was the most incongruous vessel to be plying these outsized waters. Contrary to the forecast conditions, Lake Michigan had turned into a raging fury of six-foot waves enveloping me in their deep green broiling water. When you make a bathtub into a boat, you expect to get wet, but this was way more than wet. I was beginning to fear, and rightly so, that I would be tipped over or washed out if I let my rig get broadside to the walls of water. Cascading waves had already filled the bottom of the tub and soaked me to the skin.

13

The Great and Famous Failure

As the morning sun rose higher, visibility improved and reality finally sank in—I was actually out on the big lake. The fog was dissipating, Michigan's shoreline was fading, and I was getting the hang of steering by rhythmically turning the motor in opposite directions to the fuel raft's pull. Unfortunately, due to my lack of nautical know-how, this bathtub craft was not designed to handle whitecap-topped waves of more than a couple of feet.

Reassuringly, the amateur radio communications link between the bathtub and shore hummed with traffic. My main on-shore contact was Fred Richter, amateur radio call sign W8VTM, a ham buddy I'd known since high school. He now lived in Ludington. Back then, we often talked via ham radio during lunch hours and after school for many months before we met face to face. We both currently worked in similar jobs as electronic technicians maintaining two-way radio systems.

Today, Fred was my link to the world through his two-meter VHF (146.94 MHz) transmitting and receiving equipment and my battery powered 1950's vintage 'handi-talkie' Motorola radio set. As I forged westward, I stayed in constant touch with Fred's calming voice to learn what was happening on shore. I would call, "W8VTM, this is W8BLP." Within seconds, I would hear "W8BLP, this is W8VTM, go ahead." Then I'd ask my question or make a comment to Fred on the amateur radio frequency.

In 1969, VHF radios like ours were not used for emergency marine communication. Back then, the primary channel for marine communications was a low frequency 2182 kilohertz channel monitored by ships of all sizes. It was the frequency of choice for communications on Great Lakes water. Unfortunately, communication via the low frequency marine channel was prone to interference. It also required a long, ungainly antenna and rather large and heavy electronic gear. By contrast, VHF used much smaller antennas and more compact radio gear. My choice of a two-meter (144 MHz) VHF communications frequency for a Lake Michigan crossing was considered unusual and not very practical by both the marine and amateur radio communities. Of course, those same people also deemed my choice of watercraft unsuitable.

As it turned out, my unorthodox communications system worked successfully on this attempt at a lake crossing. I was also a little ahead of my time with my choice of a VHF frequency for communications because a few years later VHF radio channels became the standard for marine use due to their technical and operational advantages. The jury is still out on the watercraft issue.

When the news media got wind I was communicating through local ham radio operators, Fred Richter was swamped with telephone calls. The reporters wanted to know what was happening out on the lake. Was I still underway? Where was I on my planned trip? Had I had any problems so far? Was the shower head still working? Little did they know just how desperate things were.

I was using a one-watt, portable, two-way radio with a small ground plane antenna fastened to the top of a 7-foot fiberglass mast, which was fastened to the top of the splash shield. It was basically a line-of-sight system. As long as the bathtub antenna was in sight of Fred's antenna, the system worked well. However, over longer distances where the curvature of the earth (or Lake Michigan waves) blocked direct line-of-sight, my low power communications with the shore became problematic.

Time passes quickly when you're busy, and I was getting busier by the minute. Within an hour of launching, I looked up to see the carferry, the one I knew my wife and father were aboard, heading out across the lake. It was several miles from me so I couldn't see anyone on the boat, and they couldn't see me. Then it occurred to me that I was quite a distance north of the carferry track, and I needed to do a better job navigating. According to my calculations, the ferry should have practically run me down if we were on the same path to Manitowoc. I took a short break from communications and steerage to contemplate this error. Since the wind had picked up, the waves were bigger, and as I moved farther out into Lake Michigan, keeping the craft on a reasonable track westward had become more difficult. And now my forward speed seemed to be slower.

Around 9 a.m. I realized that the wind and waves out of the northwest had definitely impeded my forward progress, as did the fuel raft that had never been tested on water. Towing that indispensable accessory just magnified the tub's yawing motion caused by the waves. The whole craft would skid sideways, first to one side, then to the other. In addition, the waves were now big enough that when the tub went down into the trough, I couldn't communicate with Fred just a few miles away because water blocked the radio signal. On top of a wave, I could be heard in Kewaunee, Wisconsin across the lake, by amateur radio operator Tim Selner, call sign WA9SRW.

Indeed, the wind was increasing as the minutes passed. Now several miles offshore in a relentless string of pounding waves, the bathtub craft was making almost no progress toward the west. Truly it was the most incongruous vessel to be plying these outsized waters. The constant gyrations of the tub created a scary sequence of repeated up and down and back and forth movement worthy of an amusement park stomach churner. The even more frightening aspect of this situation was that the pounding waves were getting larger and more threatening. First, I rode up the front of a wave, which I could not see because I was facing backward. Then, as I leaned my head under the splash shield, the tub would be hit by the foaming whitecap of roiling water at the top of the wave. Immediately, it would drop sharply, nose down into the next trough.

One of the most uncomfortable aspects of this motion was the sensation of falling backwards each time I dropped into the trench between waves. This stomach-wrenching freefall would come to a jolting halt at the bottom of the canyon of ominous water. Embedded in my mind is this scene of utter isolation within the fearsome turbulence. At the bottom of each wave was a moving wall of powerful green water on all sides, just inches away. Within a second or two, I knew the tub would begin the rise, first slowly and then faster and faster as I approached the foaming vertical wall at the top of each swell. Not being able to see ahead simply added to my fear that the next wave might be so big that it would completely swallow me. Fortunately, my ungainly craft was very strong. Had it not been a cast-iron bathtub with a sheet-steel splash shield, it would have been crushed by the tremendous pounding and weight of each wave as it crashed into the rig.

At any instant, I expected to be washed out of the tub and lose my communications link and likely any chance of rescue. If I were washed into the water, I would only be able to survive a few hours at most before hypothermia set in. The water in Lake Michigan in early July is not freezing, but at 60 degrees or so not warm enough to sustain life for long.

During moments near the tops of the waves, I could barely make out a shoreline in the distance before another crashing wall of water hit behind my head. Dry land was now well beyond my swimming range. There wasn't much time to think about the circumstances. All my energy was needed to keep the tub from capsizing. This might have been a good time to turn back toward shore if not for the waves coming from the northwest. If I tried to turn to the east, the whole rig would likely be tipped over sideways when the next wave hit. A down-wind run was out of the question with only two inches of freeboard where the outboard motor attached on the rear; the cold, fast moving water would likely flush me out as it overtook the tub from the rear. Traveling in any direction had become impossible.

In situations like this, one thinks of nothing except survival. My only option was to call for help. With all of the turbulence and violent movement, I was unsure I could steer the craft with one hand and use the radio at the same time. Assuming the radio actually worked, another frightening thought occurred to me: even if someone responded to my call, they might not be able to find my tiny vessel.

As the bathtub slammed into the bottom of another wave, I grabbed the microphone to the right of my head and called: "W8VTM this is W8BLP marine mobile, do you copy Fred?"

I held my breath.

No answer.

When the bathtub topped out on the next wave, I called again.

The radio was silent. And then, just as I started down into the next trough, I heard Fred answer.

Finally, over the course of several waves, I managed to tell him I was afraid of being overturned. I told him I needed help because I couldn't turn back toward shore. I was trapped. It was the bleakest and most harrowing moment of my life.

Minutes later, as I topped another wave, Fred called with word the Coast Guard was on the way. Many minutes that seemed like hours passed before I saw a boat far off to the southeast. It turned out to be the 44-foot Coast Guard Grumman UF-1G Albatross rescue craft USCG 44345. Unfortunately, my rescuers had no idea where I was or how to locate me. It took many more minutes and several exchanges with Fred while I gyrated atop successive waves before I saw the Coast Guard boat move slowly toward me. My challenge was calculating and giving Fred a relative bearing between the Coast Guard boat and my position while still fighting to remain afloat in the fierce waves and howling wind.

Eventually, these round-about communications worked, and the rescue boat got close enough to see me. At that point, the problem for both of us was that they didn't have a whole lot of practice rescuing a bathtub. But they did an outstanding job of quickly figuring out the best procedure to get a tow rope to me.

First, they maneuvered to the upwind side to shield me from the worst of the oncoming waves. The problem then was to somehow secure a tow rope between the rescue boat and my rig. Both vessels were seesawing up and down in opposing cycles. First the long rescue boat would go way above me on the crest of a wave; then, a few seconds later, I'd be looking down on them from my tiny craft atop another wave's crest. Meanwhile, we were trying to communicate by hand signals and shouting above the howling wind.

They decided to throw a rope to me, but with all the ups and downs, it was difficult for the Coast Guardsman to judge the right moment to pitch it. A bigger problem was the rope's thickness and weight. It appeared to me to be large enough and strong enough to tow a 600-foot Great Lakes freighter. Unfortunately, they tossed what seemed to be about a hundred feet of this monster rope at the exact moment I was below them. I feared the sheer weight and bulk of it would sink me. Suddenly I couldn't move. Seeing all the rope piled around and on top of me, the crewman quickly recognized the problem and hauled the rope back up. Then, a few more minutes of repositioning followed, with each vessel rhythmically trading positions of looking either up or down at the other. Finally, they threw me a smaller rope. I somehow managed to get this towline fastened to the bottom of the radio mast on the front of my bouncing tub.

After more maneuvering, as our vessels continued to trade elevations, I managed to climb onto the Coast Guard boat. Quite frankly, I have never figured out exactly how I managed this boarding move in such heavy seas and screaming wind. Based on the circumstances, it now seems impossible, but at the time it was over in a few seconds. I must have stood up in the bathtub at just the right moment. It still scares me today to think about the whole exercise. We were all mightily relieved.

The first thing the Coast Guardsman said to me was, "Step right this way, sir, we've got coffee and doughnuts waiting. We were expecting you." After all the excitement of the past few hours, I managed a sheepish grin. I was embarrassed, exhausted and mad at myself for causing the Coast Guard to make a rescue run. It took a few minutes for me to calm down and then be shown a foot and hand hold on the rolling rescue ship as it jockeyed around to tow my bathtub craft back to Ludington harbor. Once we were underway, I carried on a shouting conversation over the wind with the commander as he operated the throttles and rudder. The crew member who welcomed me aboard appeared with a cup of coffee trying valiantly to keep it from spilling in the violent rocking and pitching of the boat. Amazingly, within minutes I went from being literally immersed in a whirlpool of angry wind and waves to the relative tranquility of a rescue vessel where my biggest challenge was drinking hot coffee without spilling it.

Thankfully, it was an anticlimactic trip back to Ludington and safety. The Coast Guardsmen thought my aborted attempt to cross the lake in a bathtub was hilarious. I can only imagine that the commander's biggest concern was what exactly to write in their incident log. After 90 years of rescuing stranded mariners, it was probably the first time—and they hoped the last time—they towed something as strange as my bathtub. And they also assumed this was the last they would ever see me or my bathtub.

They were wrong, but only slightly. Toward evening, when things settled down, I made another trip to the Ludington Coast Guard station to thank my rescuers for fishing me out of the lake. They were very gracious and took the whole episode in good humor. There was some background talk about target practice with a 50-caliber gun if they had to do the rescue again. I hoped they were only joking.

The rest of that day and the next was a sad time for me, and I was pretty discouraged about the results of my efforts and the extraordinary efforts of my support team to date. I had let everyone down by misjudging so much and making stupid and avoidable mistakes. Even Paul Harvey, the nationally syndicated radio commentator, picked on me. His afternoon broadcast included a definitive, but very short statement about the fellow who attempted to sail a bathtub across Lake Michigan: "He's back."

We hauled the bathtub out of the water, put it back on the snowmobile trailer and parked it in front of Dad's house. As one would expect after such a famous attempt to cross Lake Michigan had failed, a continuous parade of cars drove by to view the now infamous bathtub sitting at the corner of Ludington and Gaylord avenues.

I was not the only one in the family on Lake Michigan that day. After their four-hour ride to Manitowoc on the ferry, Dad and Ariel rode the same ferry for another four hours back to Ludington. After a long day of traveling and hearing only second-hand reports from the ship's crew about my trials and tribulations, they arrived home at 6 p.m. When questioned by a reporter, Ariel's comment about the bathtub trip was, "I think he's goofy." It was a fitting description of my nautical misadventure from someone who knew me quite well.

In the great scheme of things, my tubbing odyssey was endowed with many totally unexpected events and helpers who materially and absolutely made a difference in furthering my aspirations. And about the time I thought the bathtub odyssey was going to end, a bolt of nautical lightning was about to strike again.

As I was getting ready to pack up the whole rig and depart for East Lansing, I noticed someone very carefully studying the bathtub as it sat at the curbside. Normally, gawkers concentrated their attention on the two-way radio or the oddball compass or maybe the geeky looking nose cones. But this guy was carefully studying the angle iron structure and how the barrels were held in place. The interested observer turned out to be 58- year-old Gerald Heslipen, Dad's next-door neighbor. Born and raised in Chicago, and married in Ludington in 1941, he had spent over 20 years on Lake Michigan as a sailor on Chesapeake and Ohio Railway Carferries. He was now a ship's captain. Unlike most of the curious onlookers, Capt. "Gerry" Heslipen wasn't pointing and laughing at the modified bathtub. He was inspecting the construction details. After a good look around, Capt. Heslipen quietly came in the house and talked with me about the day's events.

His observations were both practical and reassuring. He believed the bathtub craft could make it across the lake under the proper circumstances. He also thought my weather forecasting skills needed a significant upgrade. He went on to say that Lake Michigan can be as smooth as a table top when conditions are right. For some unknown reason, and to my good fortune, I was the benefactor of some sage advice that evening from a knowledgeable expert who wanted to see me succeed in my strange quest to cross the big lake. Capt. Heslipen urged me to be patient. Given this unruly lake's normal cycles, he said, the proper weather conditions for a lake crossing would occur later in the summer. He offered to call me when he thought the weather would be right for another bathtub trip across the lake. Although I was pretty discouraged after my harrowing experience, I was certainly willing to listen. What impressed me most in this conversation was that the nautical advice was coming from a very experienced Lake Michigan sailor who unknowingly, or maybe not so unknowingly, joined my list of volunteer advisors and mentors whose only motive was to help a crazy wild dreamer with a bizarre idea.

Overnight, my wheels started turning; maybe there could be another try. But I had lots of work to do on the navigation and fuel systems before a second trip was ever attempted. I headed back to East Lansing with the bathtub in tow—sadder, wiser and definitely the goat of all jokes. Fred Behnke would be anticipating having a super good time at my expense. And he did!

The newspapers had a field day at my ego's expense.

Lansing State Journal featured a picture of the bathtub craft with the headline: "Dub It a Flub-Man in a Tub"

Pacific Stars & Stripes, "Vic's Folly Fails Lake Test; Bathtub Sailor Finds Plan Is All Wet", July 7, 1969

The Chicago Tribune, "Tub Skipper Gives Up Trip", July 6, 1969

Detroit Free Press, "Bathtub Mariner Is All Washed Up", July 6, 1969

The *Lansing State Journal* featured a photograph of me and my bathtub craft on the front page of the Sunday edition.

I was quoted on several fronts: safety, boating, the Coast Guard, and unsafe bathtubs.

United Press International (UPI) got the story straight, sort of. I was "All Washed Up."

I was pretty discouraged about my nautical disaster. And I certainly got the "washed up" treatment from everyone, including my work mates. What I actually said was not necessarily what was quoted. I was quoted in the newspapers as saying that I shouldn't have been allowed on the lake in my bathtub craft when what I said was that some people thought I should not have been allowed on the lake, and that maybe I should have taken their advice. I had experienced a lot of living in just a few hours, including a close scrape with disaster and an aborted trip with a bad ending. I had endured a public and very frightening embarrassment along with a good dose of learning the hard way. If ever there was a time to quit and give up on making the trip across the lake, it was now.

14

Big Question: Try Again?

My anguish was given no rest at work because I had to take the razzing from everyone, fellow workers and service customers alike. I was miserable. It was not easy answering all the questions about the flubbed tub trip. I was now deemed a failure both privately and publicly. Fred Behnke, my boss, did not let any opportunity go by to request that I pay up the five bucks. My standard response to his demand was that the summer was not over. And so, life went on. Normal routines resumed at work and at home. Conventional wisdom would have been to suffer my losses, consider myself lucky to be safe and alive, and pay the five-dollar bet. But then, this was not a conventional summer.

The forlorn watercraft on the trailer in my driveway was a constant reminder of my disastrous experience. Not being one to give up easily, I turned things over and over in my mind. What had I done wrong? Was the whole idea flawed? Could I overcome my stupid mistakes, and would I live to tell the tale if I attempted to cross the lake again? I needed to be mindful of my responsibilities to my family, friends, and my job. Over many days of agonizing contemplation, I made a very careful assessment of the situation. I could not afford to make the same mistakes twice or I might pay with my life.

My informal support crew was very understanding. They were more than willing to keep on trying, and they were most forgiving of my shortcomings. I had greatly miscalculated some critical processes and made some foolish moves. But I had also learned a whole lot in a very short time about what not to do and when not to do it. My dad's continuing advice was to consider my experience a warning not to test my fate any further. Dad's reaction to the flub was understandable, but he was also someone who always persisted when the chips were down. I felt very conflicted about it all, but only I could resolve my dilemma.

After much soul searching, examining the physical evidence and evaluating my capabilities, I came to the conclusion that a successful trip across Lake Michigan in that tiny bathtub craft was indeed possible. I just had to be persistent and pay a lot more attention to details. Capt. Gerry Heslipen's encouraging advice about picking the right travel weather and making sure the bathtub craft was otherwise ready kept rattling around in my head.

In my final analysis of success and failure, I concluded you can only be successful when you never give up.

After a week or so of hanging my head and getting my psyche patched together, I started planning another go at it. The nautical education had cost me a lot of sweat and tears, and I vowed not to make any mistake twice. The little red house on Ann Street in East Lansing had a garage that could be turned into a refit and modification shipyard. How about a bathtub yard? Armed with hard-earned knowledge, I started planning the improvements to the bathtub craft needed if I was going to complete a trip across Lake Michigan.

First, I had to get rid of the fuel raft and somehow get all of the gasoline on or in the bathtub. To solve the fuel problem, the support crew and I decided to mount two 2x4 boards on brackets along each side of the flotation barrels so the five six-gallon gas cans could be tied to the top of these boards. Testing confirmed this idea would work. However, when the tanks were full with 190 pounds of gasoline, the whole craft sank dangerously deeper in the water.

This extra weight aggravated one of the original problems: the scant two inches of freeboard in the rear of the tub. If I inadvertently leaned toward the rear when the tub was fully loaded, the whole rear end, including the outboard motor, would sink under water. This presented such a precarious situation that I wouldn't be able to work on the outboard motor or even lift the cover of the motor when underway. Nevertheless, I decided to live with this risky situation knowing I would not be able to attempt even minor repairs if I had to access the outboard motor.

The next issue for consideration was my need for an inexpensive dry locker that was light weight and waterproof. Someone suggested I use a 30-gallon plastic garbage container and place it in the rear of the bathtub. My legs and feet would go alongside the container, and I would ride in an inclined position with my head mostly underneath the sheet-steel splash shield. The snap on, relatively watertight lid of the garbage can was easy to remove and everything inside the container was easily accessible to me by just bending over slightly. It was a poor man's solution to a vexing problem. I put the heavy marine battery in the bottom of this container to keep it dry and close to the engine for the electric start; its weight ensured the garbage can would not wash overboard in heavy seas unless the wave was big enough to take me and the trash container both out.

Finally, the most noteworthy communication improvement I made was to borrow and install Don Hewson's full-size Motorola two-way radio. I put the transmitter-receiver unit in the plastic garbage can and mounted the control head and microphone under the forward splash shield. Although this radio consumed quite a bit of 12-volt power from the battery, it had 25 watts of transmitter output power, a vast improvement over the single watt portable I used on the aborted mission.

Only a true friend would loan his expensive two-way radio for use on a bathtub craft with a checkered history of failure. Don's loan of equipment and labor was typical of my support team. Because of their generous ways and encouraging advice and help, I was able to move on with my plan for another try at the big lake. Don had faith that his radio would be returned. If things turned out so badly that the radio was lost, I assumed he would be able to recover his loss from my estate.

Another friend, Chuck Ogle at Custom Electronics, located at the Lansing airport, convinced me to try using a VHF "omni" aircraft receiver on the bathtub. This device would indicate the direction of Manitowoc, Wisconsin when I was on the lake. I also experimented with a regular AM car radio that used a ferrite loop antenna mounted on the VHF antenna mast. The ferrite loop antenna was quite directional and would allow me to direction-find broadcast signals and, therefore, determine the direction of broadcast stations. All these improvements to the tub boat were made in late July while I waited for suitable weather on Lake Michigan.

A local newspaper reporter called in mid-July to interview me for a follow-up story on my famous flub in Lake Michigan. When I mentioned that maybe I wasn't through after all, I made headlines again. I had planned to keep my mouth shut and publicity non-existent so that no one but close friends and family would be the wiser if I failed again. Now the cat was out of the bag, and I had to live with the consequences.

Newspaper Headline
"Vic's Folly Skipper to Sail Again"
Lansing State Journal
July 16, 1969, Lansing, Michigan

Meanwhile, I returned to my job doing maintenance and repair of two-way radio systems and learned to endure the continued 'tub flub' questions and jokes from clients and customers. And while I continued to plan the August re-try of the lake crossing, world events kept the public's attention focused elsewhere: Apollo 11 astronauts made man's first landing on the moon July 20, and the war in Vietnam raged amid growing controversy.

I was anxious to try out the new craft in rough water, especially the new gas tank arrangement. Could I manage to change hoses between the various top-mounted tanks while keeping the engine running. I discovered the engine would continue to run for approximately 40 seconds with the fuel hose disconnected. This sounds like ample time to change a simple push-on connector, but time flies when you're under duress rocking in the waves and your hands are slippery.

15

Testing in the Straits of Mackinac
(pronounced "mack-in-awe")

With August fast approaching, I was finally able to locate a body of water where I could do some real-world testing of my tubcraft's new navigation systems under conditions similar to those I would encounter on my next Lake Michigan trial. The crew agreed that the Straits of Mackinac might be ideal. This five-mile wide, deep-water shipping channel created by nature around 10,000 years ago between Lake Huron and Lake Michigan would provide the rough waves and treacherous currents needed for a reliable test. And the crew could observe me in the channel from the giant "Mighty Mac" suspension bridge spanning the Straits.

On the first Saturday in August, joined by my brother-in-law, Dave Haddrill, a Michigan State University student, and my friend and fellow ham radio operator Greg Hiscock, we hitched up the borrowed snowmobile trailer and headed north for the critical test. Trying to maintain a low public profile in case something went wrong, we slipped quietly away from East Lansing for the four-hour drive to Mackinaw City. I certainly didn't need to provide any more 'failed sailor' fodder for the news media.

Being a low budget operation, on Saturday evening we parked in a wooded area a few miles south of Mackinaw City and slept there instead of renting a motel room. Fortunately, we were blessed with a relatively warm, brilliantly clear and starry night. But, bloodthirsty mosquitoes were out in force.

Launch Day dawned bright and clear. This time there would be no fog and no crowds. We drove into Mackinaw City for breakfast and the launch of "Vic's Folly" on Lake Huron west of the ferry terminals. At the launch site, we eventually got everything hooked up and the tub floating with the fuel cans tied in their new arrangement to the barrel-mounted 2x4 boards. Recalling my disastrous experience towing a fuel-heavy raft, I was anxious to test this new system. If any problems showed up, helpers were standing by. When all systems were working and I could talk to Greg on the new two-way radio, I started the motor and headed north across the Straits toward St. Ignace.

Our initial conversation, with Greg on his portable radio in the moving car and me underway in the bathtub rig, went something like this:

"WA8DLI mobile, this is W8BLP marine mobile, underway on the Straits, how do you read my signal?"

His surprising response:

"W8BLP marine mobile, this is WA8DLI mobile: I read you loud and clear. We are waiting in downtown Mackinaw City until you are out in the deep-water channel before we start across the bridge."

In our planning for this little venture, we had forgotten that the Mackinac Bridge Authority doesn't allow vehicles to stop anywhere on the bridge. Dave and Greg would not be able to observe my voyage in the water below except while moving. But they would be in constant radio contact. I replied that everything was working fine and I would continue to radio my position as I went along.

In addition to the normal tasks of keeping a straight course and watching out for other vessels, I inspected all the newly rigged hoses and cables and checked for leaks. The repositioned fuel tanks worked well, and Don Hewson's two-way radio was performing perfectly. How different this was from my first trip! I was pleased to discover the bathtub watercraft was finally working the way it was designed to work. Within the hour, I was approaching the St. Ignace shoreline.

Greg informed me there was a marina to the west of the bridge, opposite the side I was on, so I headed there, navigating under a small bridge in the northernmost section of the causeway. I landed at the small marina and was greeted by the owner who came out to marvel at my bizarre rig. She also bragged she herself had made an epic journey: a midwinter round trip across the ice with a dog sled and team of dogs. She became, she said, the first and possibly only woman ever to achieve this distinction. I have yet to verify her name or her story.

Once Dave and Greg showed up and learned how smoothly everything was going, I was anxious to make the trip back to Mackinaw City. The route this time would take me southeast directly under the 155-foot high main span of the bridge and between its 550-foot tall suspension towers. This time, because of the earlier crossing, spectators were waiting for a closer look-see. Traffic not only slowed, but some cars stopped so occupants could watch as the tub cruised under the bridge to the east side. Because of the currents, the waves and the many large ships using the deep-water channel, my crossing was not as easy as I had imagined. I had to be especially careful not to be in the channel when one of those freighters was in the area. Some are over 1,000 feet long and would not be able to stop if I capsized.

After all my previous troubles on Lake Michigan, this trip was a breeze with everything working as planned. Our conversation on the drive home was animated and lively, with many jokes about hassling Fred Behnke for the five dollars. We were now ready to take on Lake Michigan.

Curiously, a day later (August 4, 1969), a photo of me in the tub craft squarely under the Mackinac Bridge appeared in the Lansing State Journal. I am still puzzled about how they obtained that picture because I never saw anyone anywhere taking photos. In the accompanying article, reporter Rita Rice reveals to Lansing readers that "Lansing's only bathtub sailor made a successful trial run across the Mackinac Straits Sunday.

Newspaper headline:
"Tub Gassed to Go"
"Trial Run in Mackinac Straits Pleases Area
Skipper—Now On to Lake Michigan"
Lansing State Journal
August 4, 1969, Lansing, Michigan

16

Waiting for the Weather

I parked the trailer with the bathtub in my garage in East Lansing and resigned myself to waiting for proper weather for bathtub boating on Lake Michigan. As the days of August ticked by, the world pretty well forgot about my bathtub boat, but I was still being teased regularly at work by Fred Behnke to pay up the wager. I spent evenings in the garage tinkering in anticipation of giving the trip one last try before autumn.

Finally, on Friday evening August 22, I received the long - awaited weather call from Capt. Gerry Heslipen. He told me he expected the next three or four days to be ideal conditions for another try on the big lake. His primary criteria for good sailing were now in place: an atmospheric high-pressure zone over Lake Michigan and no storms or bad weather within 500 miles. Of all the help and encouragement I received in this venture, my fortuitous encounter with Capt. Gerry Heslipen was the most influential and pivotal. As he said on the night my first attempt failed, weather is the key to navigating Lake Michigan.

Immediately after his call, I called Dad to let him know to expect me in Ludington Saturday night. I'd use his house again as my base of operations, knowing full well he'd be less than thrilled to have me out on the lake. More than once that summer, he had reminded me of my prior failure. My next call was to Gordon Forgar. As a keenly interested observer of the bathtub venture, he had promised to accompany me in a 19-foot speed boat across the lake. I also called Fred Behnke and told him I'd miss work on Monday. He expressed no surprise about my new plan and wished me luck on the big bet.

Taking advantage of lessons learned, I kept these new plans to myself and my team of nautical neophytes. I wanted to avoid another media fiasco but, more importantly, I didn't want the Coast Guard to stop me from embarking on the trip. And, this time the wife and kids would stay at home.

As I drove toward Ludington, questions and self-doubts ran amok in my mind. Should I turn back and forget the whole thing? Could the weather forecast be wrong and I'd find myself battling high winds and heavy seas? What if I got swamped and overturned? What if the Coast Guard decided to stop me? What would happen to my kids if I disappeared on Lake Michigan? These were certainly not new thoughts; nonetheless, the painful reality of my recent failure burned in my mind. Images of those large boiling waves and walls of green water engulfing me still chilled me to my bones.

Although the liabilities were enormous, my anxiety slowly drained away as I reviewed key facts: the bathtub craft of angle iron, threaded steel rods, cast iron, and sheet steel was extremely sturdy; I had confidence and hard-won experience in what it could do and how it would hold together; I had planned for emergencies, tested equipment, and carefully planned for the trip. If I failed it would be because something else went wrong, not because I didn't try.

When I arrived in Ludington, I quickly backed the rig into Dad's garage. No point stirring up the neighborhood on a Saturday afternoon. Later, in the early evening, I pulled the whole rig down the street to a gas station to fill up all five tanks and to make sure the gasoline/oil mixture was proper for the outboard engine. The minute I pulled into the gas station; a small crowd gathered to take a look. I went about my business and tried to be as nonchalant as possible as the gathering crowd made wisecracks.

Saturday evening passed at my father's house with visits from Capt. Heslipen, who reaffirmed the weather, and a few well-wishers wanting to take a last look at the beast in the garage.

My father devoted his time to trying once more to convince me the trip was too dangerous to undertake. He again pointed out my disastrous experience in July and the high risk of trying again. However, although this was a thought-provoking time for me, Dad knew I would not back down no matter what he said. There was no turning back.

I went to bed with a whirlwind of thoughts racing around in my head. I had dreams of large waves, laughing crowds of people jeering at me and pointing to my ungainly craft, and even the Coast Guard pulling me out of the bathtub and shooting it full of holes until it sank in a whirlpool of boiling water and steam. I imagined myself alone in the middle of Lake Michigan with only a gas can to cling to as the tub sank into the depths. I dreamed of large newspaper headlines screaming "failure, failure, failure." There were groups of people standing around saying, "I knew he couldn't do it. He shouldn't have tried such a dangerous stunt." It was a fitful night of tossing and turning, waiting for morning and my adventure to play out.

17

Sunday, August 24, 1969

Suddenly my dad was standing over me shaking my shoulder, saying, "Vic, it's time to get up." It was 5:00 a.m., Sunday, August 24, 1969.

I had requested the pre-dawn wake up so I could be ready and launched at first light. Dad insisted I eat a decent breakfast. He pointed out once again that it might be my last. Eggs, toast, juice, and a sip of hot chocolate went down in a gulp, then I hurried out to the garage to hook up the trailer for the short trip to the new public boat-launching ramp on Lake Michigan. It was only a few hundred feet from the Ludington Coast Guard Station. I was hoping they wouldn't notice.

The new launch was built to accommodate increasing numbers of salmon and lake trout fisherman. These large game fish had been introduced to the Great Lakes only a few years earlier to solve problems with alewives and sea lampreys overtaking native fish populations. The plantings were a huge success, and by the fall of 1969, Coho salmon were being caught in increasing numbers off Ludington. As a result, I found myself that Saturday morning launching my bathtub rig with a bunch of hopeful fishermen. Their fishing boats were all bigger by far than my bizarre vessel. Some of the fishermen may even have thought my tub was some new form of fishing apparatus about to be loaded aboard a fishing boat. Generally, boats used for fishing on Lake Michigan are at least 15 feet or longer because of the larger waves and the possibility of fast approaching storms. This generality about boat size was the basis of my bet with Fred Behnke and our disagreement about minimum size needed for a craft to cross Lake Michigan.

As crazy as my bathtub craft may have seemed to the world that morning, something unusual caught my eye. I was in the boat slip next to a man and his young daughter who were preparing a canoe for a trip out on the lake to try their luck at fishing. Now, this man was not the first or the last to go out in Lake Michigan in a canoe, but I thought to myself that as crazy as my bathtub craft might seem, at least I was prepared for the worst. The last I saw of the father-daughter team, they were chugging out between the break walls into the big lake with their one horsepower motor humming along. When telling the canoe story later, I said, "I may be crazy, but I'm not stupid." Many people still disagree with my statement.

About this time, Gordon Forgar and his nephew arrived at the launch ramp with his boat in tow and very sleepy eyes. They had driven since the wee hours from Lansing to get to Ludington for the bathtub launch and they were ready to accompany me on the big trip.

Dad had been urging me from the time I got out of bed to top off the tanks with fuel. I had brought along an extra tank as a spare so that I could prepare the gas/oil mixture that the outboard engine required. I kept telling him I had enough fuel to go for 12 hours, and that the trip would only take 10 hours and that I had plenty of gas in reserve. Dad was paying very close attention to my estimates of running time and fuel. So, after everything else was taken care of, I reluctantly agreed to top off all five gas tanks and make sure they were completely and absolutely full, just to keep Dad happy. Little did I know that I might be very thankful later in the day that he had been so insistent.

While I was busy making these last-minute preparations and checking everything out, Dad was asking me when he should notify rescue authorities if I had a problem. My attention was so focused on my own preparations that I paid little attention to him even when he told me: "If you don't show up in Manitowoc by 5 p.m. this afternoon, I'll call out a search and rescue mission."

Finally, it was time to go. It was a beautiful Sunday morning with little wind, no waves, and as warm as one can expect early in the day in late summer. The tub was launched and waiting. I had given my car keys to Dad, donned my life jacket ready to begin the trip, and noticed a few people standing around watching me prepare to go. Dad had one final instruction that served me well later that day. He said that the first thing I would see of Manitowoc, Wisconsin would be the large grain elevator located on the lake shore near the carferry docks. It is a very tall building with a rotating aircraft beacon on top that can be seen for many miles out on the lake. I mentally filed dad's last instruction away, figuring my first goal was to find Wisconsin, then I would worry about finding Manitowoc.

With a last wave of my hand, I twisted the throttle on the outboard engine and headed out toward the channel between the breakwalls. I was on my way.

Photo credit: Russ Miller, Ludington Daily News

With 190 pounds of gasoline stacked around me, the rear gas cans partially in the water and the rear of the bathtub dangerously close to submerging, there was no room for error or miscalculation.

I checked in on the two-way radio with Fred Richter who had risen early and was on communications duty again for this second try. Now, for the second time this summer, the Ludington ham radio community would be my vital lifeline of communications. As I left the harbor, I was talking to Fred with almost the same clarity as a telephone conversation. When passing through the channel between the lighthouses, the water swells suddenly became much longer, and the water took on deeper and more vivid color as I entered the big lake. I was both excited and apprehensive as I contemplated the circumstances of being out on Lake Michigan in any small craft, let alone a tiny bathtub. Fortunately, this Sunday morning, the weather was calm, the sun was shining, and the swells were gentle. At this moment, Capt. Heslipen's weather forecast was perfect.

Following 100 yards behind me was Gordon Forgar in his speed boat. It was reassuring to know that rescue or help was on hand if I needed it. I noticed the sun was rising directly over the city of Ludington, so navigation was relatively easy. By keeping the sun directly over the outboard motor, I would be making a straight track across the lake like the carferries.

This was a navigational error that I would severely regret later in the day.

It was one of those idyllic but infrequent Michigan water days. The weather was so good that many boats were moving around on the lake looking for fish or just enjoying a cruise. I didn't want to run into one of them, but my forward visibility was very restricted by both my reclining position and the high splash shield. Although I had mounted a marine mirror on one side it was very ineffective for spotting other boats. So, periodically, I leaned around the splash shield to take stock. After some minutes of running uneventfully, and a mile or so out on the lake, Gordon and his nephew pulled alongside and said they were going back into Ludington for breakfast. They'd return and rendezvous with me a little later since I could go no more than six miles per hour; his craft would do 30 mph. "No problem," I replied. That was the last time I saw Gordon until I stopped at his boat sales yard in Lansing some days later. It wasn't that Gordon didn't try to find me after breakfast. They searched for several hours, he said, but didn't realize how tiny my bathtub craft really was, and how vast Lake Michigan really is.

Shortly after my departure from Ludington, a most unusual safety message was broadcast by the Coast Guard to all ships on Lake Michigan. The 2182 Kilohertz common channel was monitored by all watercraft that were radio equipped, so that initial communications could be established between ships or for use in emergencies. Occasionally, the Coast Guard would also broadcast messages of common interest concerning the safety of all watercraft in the area. These safety messages were always broadcast in a serious manner befitting their concern for the safety of life and property. However, on this beautiful, sunny Sunday morning, I was told a few days later that the Coast Guardsman reading the message quickly began to suffer from the giggles as he attempted to advise all shipping on Lake Michigan to be on the lookout for a white and orange bathtub crossing Lake Michigan between Ludington, Michigan and Manitowoc, Wisconsin.

I'm sure as he read the safety message he was imagining the captain of a gigantic lake freighter steaming along in the middle of Lake Michigan passing my tiny bathtub and waving nonchalantly while looking for the shower head and the soap. Rumors persisted that more than one ship's captain and crew had some humorous conversations that morning after hearing the Coast Guard's safety message. According to reliable witnesses, the manner in which the safety message was delivered, giggles and all, was as funny as the message itself. Days later, I was told by carferry crewmen that all who heard it kept hoping they would catch sight of the floating bathtub. Quite frankly, I had been hoping they didn't know I was out there.

A few miles out of Ludington, I spotted a boat sitting calmly in the water with only a small boy visible on the rear deck. He was straining to see what kind of craft I was in. As I neared the vessel, the boy suddenly darted below deck. Just as I passed off their stern, the boy and his parents appeared topside to take a startled look. I waved and settled back nonchalantly into my reclining position. That boat was the last watercraft I saw for several hours on my way out of Ludington.

Suddenly, I was startled out of complacent reverie by the crashing down of my antenna mast. The adjustable ball holding the bottom of the mast to the top of the splash shield had broken. Fortunately, I could simply prop the mast upright with no noticeable degradation of the two-way radio signal. Except for that minor incident, my bathtub craft was running well, the two-way radio kept me in contact with Fred Richter, and the long, gentle swells allowed me to take a look at my surroundings. Some time ago I had completely lost sight of land. Now there was nothing to see. It was an awesome but somewhat disquieting feeling to realize you are totally alone surrounded by nothing but water and sky. My only guide to where I was and where I wanted to go was the rising sun and my own intuition.

I was quite confident that all I needed to do was steer toward what I thought was west.

Unfortunately, I was not paying enough attention to my magnetic compass. That task had somehow just slipped off my mental "to do" list. Because the bathtub was more or less waddling through the water, the compass needle was skipping around too, and took some extra effort to read even an approximate bearing. Meanwhile, the radio was keeping me occupied with constant chatter. I was waiting for Fred Rechter to set up a phone patch for me, which was also distracting. (A phone patch is a connection between the landline telephone network and the ham radio transmitting and receiving equipment that would let me talk to someone Fred called.)

During one of my earliest conversations with Mayor Graves of Lansing, I jokingly promised that since he was not going with me on this trip, I would give him a call if I ever got to the middle of Lake Michigan. Since I had been underway for several hours I assumed I must be near the middle. And since it was late Sunday morning, I asked Fred to try to contact Mayor Graves by phone. I really never expected Fred to actually get the mayor to take my call, nor do I know how he obtained the number. But a few minutes later I was talking to his Honor, the Mayor. Of course, being on a common ham radio frequency, every able-bodied amateur radio operator within many miles was listening to my call. I think the Mayor was more than a little surprised also to actually hear from me out in the middle of Lake Michigan. And I'm willing to bet big bucks the retired Merchant Marine captain has not conversed with a more unusual watercraft before or since. It was a short but memorable conversation just before noon of a spectacular day.

All my makeshift systems were working well. I easily switched the fuel hoses going to the outboard motor to balance the fuel weight, and my communications system worked perfectly. Despite a slight breeze out of my perceived westerly direction, I had confidence in Capt. Heslipen's weather forecast. Based on my estimated running time, I knew I must be halfway across the lake.

18

Navigation Problems and a Dying Battery

Having ended the conversation with the mayor, I twisted my body around to take a look in my forward direction. This time I spotted a ship, a large ship, several miles distant. I recognized it as a carferry, but it was going in a strange direction, on a path almost perpendicular to my course. My first reaction was that I was hallucinating. Had I finally gone over the edge? Was I headed for nowhere in the middle of Lake Michigan? The answer to my anguished questions turned out to be both 'no' and 'yes.' Confusion ran rampant in my mind.

After a few seconds of contemplation and rising panic, I reported my sighting to Fred. To confirm it, he immediately called the Chesapeake and Ohio Carferry dock in Ludington to inquire as to the whereabouts of their ships at that moment. We both assumed that I was seeing one of their boats and that, somehow, I had navigated to a position that would explain the direction the unknown carferry was taking with respect to my course. After a few minutes of silence, Fred came back on the radio to report that all of the Chesapeake and Ohio Carferries based in Ludington were in port at that moment. The news was unbelievable. I decided to take another look around to see if the eerie ship was still there. It was!

Needless to say, I was more than a little excited by this time. In fact, I was sure my mind was playing tricks on me. I was alone, scared, under tremendous pressure and this ghost carferry was the result. I decided to dig out my camera to take a picture. I wanted to be able to prove later, if I lived, whether I was seeing things or not. The radio had been silent for a few minutes when Fred excitedly came back on the air; he knew that the Ann Arbor Railroad also operated a ferry between Frankfort and Manitowoc, Wisconsin. Fred had called the Ann Arbor Railroad ferry office to inquire if maybe they had a ferry out on Lake Michigan somewhere. Sure enough, the reply came back that 'yes' they did have a ferry on the lake. It was reported to be approximately mid-lake on a southwesterly course on a direct line between Frankfort and Manitowoc. If I was seeing that ferry then, according to Fred and his Frankfort contact, I must be way off course and headed in a northerly direction up the middle of Lake Michigan to nowhere in particular except open lake.

It seemed impossible that I could have navigated so far from my intended course. But the whole subject was still suspect unless some additional concrete evidence of my sighting could be obtained. So, a roundabout communication followed with Fred on the telephone to the Ann Arbor Carferry dispatcher in Frankfort who then contacted the ferry by radio. The ferry captain was asked to look in my direction to see if anyone on the boat could see me. I am sure some considerable interest was generated among the crew on that ship straining to catch a glimpse of my little day-glow orange and white craft. The word came back that I was not in sight. This left the question of positive identification of the carferry open. And posed the even bigger question: Where in the blazes was I?

The ungainly communications network hummed for a few minutes until the ferry's captain came up with the simple solution. He would blow the whistle on his ship. Even if they couldn't see me, I would be able to identify them. A few seconds later, I heard the distant low moan of the whistle. I was elated, but at the same time completely devastated. The good news was that I knew fairly accurately where I was. The bad news was obvious; I was a considerable distance off course in the middle of Lake Michigan. Through our roundabout communications, the captain then inquired whether I would want them to turn around and attempt to pick me up. It was a wonderful gesture on his part, but I was still running well, I now knew where I was, and I was not about to quit just because I was a 'little' off course.

Many moons later, I would think about the offer to be picked up by the ferry, and wonder—given the circumstances—if I was a crazy fool not to accept that possibly life-saving invitation. I could have made everybody on that Ann Arbor ferry very excited indeed to see firsthand what a real nut case in a floating bathtub looks like!

As the now identified carferry motored out of sight on the horizon, I began to take stock of my fuel situation. I knew I was approximately 45 miles from Manitowoc, that my current navigation procedures were worthless, and that if I was really lucky I had perhaps enough fuel to travel 30 miles at best. The only thing I had going for me was sheer determination and dumb luck. The time was around noon, so I had about eight hours of daylight left, plenty of time to get to Manitowoc if I navigated without error and didn't run out of fuel.

As if I didn't already have enough problems to contend with suddenly I detected another. When I keyed the microphone on the two-way radio, the push-to-talk relay would hesitate a moment before engaging. My experience as a radio technician told me instantly what was wrong. My battery was going dead! The big marine battery in the bottom of the plastic garbage container was obviously not being charged by the generator on the outboard motor. I quickly made the decision to save whatever power was left in the battery for a real emergency. I shut down the omni aircraft radio immediately. Then I made one short call to Fred on shore to let him know my battery was going dead, that I was shutting down the two-way radio and that I would call again when either I ran out of fuel or I spotted Manitowoc. I never waited for a response, just turned off everything electrical connected to the battery.

Later, I surmised that the outboard motor wasn't running fast enough to let the generator charge the battery. This problem was probably caused by the pitch of the propeller being too great for the load an inefficient bathtub waddling through the water imposed on the outboard engine. Even at full throttle, the engine couldn't turn over fast enough. The result was a dying battery.

The gentle splashing of water against the tub and the steady hum of the outboard motor were now my only companions. In more normal circumstances, and from the perspective of rational thinking, I would have had time to contemplate the seriousness of the situation. I had recently passed up what was likely to be my only chance for rescue, the radio battery was dead, I was way off course, and it appeared likely that I did not have enough fuel to get to Wisconsin. The feelings of loneliness, despair, and hopelessness in that moment cannot be adequately described.

Because my situation involved multiple crises, I didn't have time to think about each one individually or rationally. The first order of business was to get my navigation under control. I needed to be able to go in a straight line, whatever direction that was, toward Manitowoc. Navigating by keeping the sun over the outboard motor was a dumb thing to do. Now I was really paying the price of ignorance.

About this time, I remembered that I had packed away an aeronautical sectional chart of the upper Lake Michigan area in my dry box, the plastic garbage container. It was loaned to me by Chuck Ogle for use with the omni-range aircraft radio. The radio had not worked at all so far on the trip, but the map was invaluable. This vintage 1969 aeronautical chart listed AM radio stations, their frequency and showed their approximate location. I also remembered that my friend Brian Monaghan had loaned me a portable AM radio to bring along. It was battery powered and had the standard broadcast as well as some shortwave, bands on it. When I packed it aboard, I thought I might be monitoring the 2182 kHz emergency marine frequency in use at that time.

Unlike most portable radios, this one had a signal strength meter that showed the relative strength of a radio signal being received. Because of my radio background, both amateur and commercial, I quickly figured out a way to determine the direction of AM radio stations in Manitowoc and elsewhere in Wisconsin with respect to my present location. I would use the signal strength meter and the directional characteristics of the radio's built-in antenna. The antenna on the portable radio was a ferrite rod about 4 inches long, wound with the wire used for the antenna. I knew that when either end of this ferrite rod pointed toward the originating radio signal, the signal strength would 'null out,' that is, the meter would read zero, and the radio station signal would just be static over the speaker. Conversely, the radio signal was strongest when the ferrite rod was perpendicular to the radio station.

Using the aircraft sectional chart to obtain that station's frequency and the portable radio to pinpoint the actual location of the broadcast station, I created a crude but effective navigation system born of acute necessity and my ham radio background; it was also a case of thinking logically and clearly while trying to keep my panic and fear under control.

I quickly discovered that I could lay the radio between the edge of the bathtub and the splash shield. This placement meant that the end of the radio case was pointing directly ahead of the bathtub. Then, by tuning the radio to a station in Manitowoc, I could swing the bathtub back and forth until the signal disappeared completely on the signal strength meter. Under this condition, I was either going directly toward or directly away from the broadcast signal when the signal disappeared. Using the compass and the sun as a very rough guide, I hoped I was going toward the signal, not in the opposite direction.

As if being lost, alone, and running low on fuel with a dead battery wasn't bad enough, I was doing all this navigational learning while floating in a semi-reclined position in a cramped bathtub craft without a keel. Simultaneously, I also had to monitor a fuel system that required constant attention. My definition of 'busy' took on a whole new meaning.

By experimenting, I had discovered that the magnetic compass would allow me to maintain a rough heading within 20 degrees or so. That old aircraft compass actually worked quite well under the constant yawing and pitching of the bathtub. Although the whole system was makeshift, considering my options, it seemed very effective.

Being without any means of communicating with shore contacts didn't deter me from trying to locate my position on the lake with this homemade navigation system. Using a combination of radio stations, the sectional chart, and the compass, I eventually calculated a rough triangulation of my position to ensure that I was making progress toward my destination.

Desperately hoping I had underestimated my fuel reserves, I decided to continue directly to Manitowoc rather than a closer point in Wisconsin. After all, I had declared getting to Manitowoc as my goal to everyone, and no small problem like a lack of fuel was going to stop me. Later in the day, when I lost all hope of ever getting there, I would wish I had just headed for the nearest shore when I had the opportunity. Regret is a great teacher if you live to see another day.

19

Alone in the Middle of Lake Michigan

The afternoon progressed with sunny skies, no breeze and very small swells. The water was absolutely smooth for long periods of time, as Capt. Heslipen had predicted it would be. My only company was an occasional seagull. Weather conditions were serene and calm; good fortune for a tiny bathtub and a lone sailor on a reckless mission. The stress of one crisis after another and constantly paying attention to steering the craft was beginning to take its toll on me both mentally and physically.

For the first time since very early morning, I realized I was physically exhausted. But there was no respite from the desperate activities of fuel monitoring, navigation, looking for land or boat of any sort, and staying alert for anything that might go wrong. I couldn't relax for even an instant. If I let go of the steering arm, the whole rig would yaw in one direction or another. Optimism was fading fast. The fuel was dwindling down. I had no outside confirmation that my navigation was anywhere near accurate. I felt more and more hopeless and desperate out on the open water.

The only sound I had heard for several hours was the motor's steady drone. My only view was a vast expanse of water in all directions. The reality of my situation emphasized just how lonely and isolated I was, more than I had ever been. That's when I talked to my mother. It was a conversation as plain and clear as I had ever had with her. I asked my question out loud into the emptiness and total serenity of the lake with both fear and disgust: "What do I do now, Ma?" I was scared, lonely, and worn down by the constant tension. I was disgusted at my self-made predicament and fearful of the unknown.

In a startling instant in this isolated setting, my mother answered in a calm and steady voice that I can still hear to this day: "Keep going toward Manitowoc, you're going to make it." Her voice was so clear and unexpected that I blurted out my answer before I could think about it: "Thanks, Ma," I replied.

For a few moments my logical, skeptical mind just went numb, unable to comprehend what had just happened. But the result was a startling rejuvenation of my enthusiasm for a successful voyage. I had gained some new confidence. Just seven months earlier, Dad had arrived home for lunch one day in January, and found Mom on the living room floor where she had died of an apparent stroke. Her funeral was a traumatic and trying time for me and this voyage, in some ways, was my rebuttal.

Within a few minutes, the enormity and total illogic of the moment struck me. I quickly twisted around looking in all directions. I was sure a boat must be nearby and someone was playing a trick on me. But there was no boat and I was alone in a world of blue-green water and light blue sky. This stark reality brought me back to the demands of the unstable craft and to another attempt at a radio navigation check.

Many years later, I still cannot explain this surreal event in rational terms. The only conclusion to be drawn is that the unexplained and unexpected is always waiting around the corner.

Along with navigation, I periodically alternated the fuel from each of my five portable fuel tanks to balance the weight between the two sides of the tub. Because of their relatively high position when they were full, balancing the weight load was critical just to maintain stability and minimize the craft's yawing motion. However, as the gas cans became emptier, I focused on keeping the amount of fuel in each tank relatively the same for an entirely different reason. I needed to use every last drop in each tank without any one tank going entirely empty. Because of the extremely small space and instability of my craft I lacked the ability to simply pour all the remaining fuel into one tank.

During one of my frequent fuel hose changes, it dawned on me that the outboard motor was an electric start engine. It did have a manual pull rope, but I had not tested it. If I failed to make the fuel hose change in time, or if I let a fuel tank run dry, the engine would quit. And if that happened, with a now dead battery, I would be forced to use the manual pull cord for a restart. However, to access the manual pull cable, I would have to unlatch the engine's top cover and reach in to grab the cable handle. On land, this was possible. In the water, however, if I leaned back toward the motor, the whole engine would sink deep enough that the top would be submerged. I was quite sure that it wouldn't start with the top under water, so I kept track of the amount of fuel in each tank very carefully and was very careful when changing fuel hoses.

It was during all this thinking about my fuel situation that I dropped a fuel hose in the water inside the tub. I was changing hoses again, which I had been doing routinely for the last 10 hours or so. After disconnecting the hose going to the engine, I had about 40 seconds to get the next hose hooked up. As I pushed the fitting onto the engine, it slipped and dropped into the standing water. Panic began to rise as I struggled to pick up the hose and get the water cleaned off and get it mated onto the engine fitting. In my haste, I dropped it again. Seconds ticked by. My hands were slippery from spilled gasoline and my mind was screaming with alarm. Finally, after what seemed like an eternity, I managed to get the fitting cleaned out with a mighty puff of air and back on the engine. The outboard continued to hum and push the bathtub along, oblivious of the desperate struggle that had just ensued.

20

Losing Hope, Seeing the Light

It was now very late in the afternoon and miraculously, I was still underway. But the fuel situation was becoming more and more critical. I could pick up each tank easily with one hand. Even if I did spot land soon, I feared I would run out of fuel before I could reach the shore.

During one of my scans of the horizon, I spotted an airplane flying at a couple of thousand feet altitude at a leisurely pace some distance from me. It appeared to be some kind of amphibious craft. Even though I was glad to see a vestige of the real world, I was so busy with the fuel and navigation that I quickly lost track of it. I later found out that it may have been one of the Coast Guard's airplanes dispatched to look for me after Dad's call that afternoon. He had said that if he didn't hear from me by 5 p.m. he was going to call for a rescue. According to Dad in a conversation the next day, the Coast Guard dispatched an aircraft and ships in the late afternoon to early evening, but all failed to spot me.

It was now after 8 p.m. Eastern time as the sun began to set in the western sky. I took note of some low clouds on the western horizon. At first I thought I was seeing land, but as the sun disappeared behind the clouds it became clear no land was in sight. Because I had so wanted to see land, the sun and clouds had created a mirage in my mind. Fortunately, I was still making progress through the water, which was very calm with no wind and almost no swells.

Dad's last words as I departed Ludington echoed in my mind: Look for the light on the grain elevator in Manitowoc. I kept twisting around in my reclining position to look toward the setting sun, but all I could see were clouds and water.

Then, just minutes after the sun set behind the clouds, around 8:40 p.m., I thought I saw a light flash on the horizon. It caught my attention, but then I didn't see anything more as my eyes strained to see something, anything. But there was nothing there. I had reached the point of desperation. Maybe the flicker of light was another apparition? I wondered what else I had seen earlier that might have been apparitions? Obviously, between the stress and the long day on the lake, my eyes were playing tricks on me. To force a modicum of calm over my rising panic, I decided to wait several minutes—an eternity—before looking around again. The minutes dragged slowly by as my desire to look for the fleeting light grew. Finally, I turned around and strained to focus my eyes on the horizon. I could see nothing but water and clouds. Suddenly, I thought I saw a flash of light! A few seconds later I thought I saw another flash! I was so excited I could hardly contain myself. I was relatively certain that I had Manitowoc in sight! It was almost celebration time!

And then the reality of the situation struck me. Thoughts whirled around in my head that I was going to run out of fuel before I got to Manitowoc, and everyone would say that I was a failure again! In my mind, just getting in sight of Manitowoc was proof that the bathtub craft could navigate Lake Michigan. I estimated that I was probably less than six miles from my goal, less than an hour's running time. I quickly turned on the two-way radio and waited a short warm-up period. Then, without listening further, I keyed the microphone and shouted that I was within sight of Manitowoc, but I didn't know if I had enough fuel to make it in. The battery was now completely dead. I couldn't hear any replies.

Now started the maddening torture of expecting the engine to run out of fuel and quit at any time. I began to plan what I would do in that situation. I could wait until it was fully dark and try to attract a passing boat with a flare. I also imagined myself sitting alone, drifting in the bathtub overnight, and hoping I could attract a passing boat in the morning. I also envisioned a carferry running over me in the middle of the night and never realizing what had happened. Although the rest of my body was exhausted, my imagination bounded into overdrive.

21

Goal in Sight, Disaster Lurking

I learned later that my last broadcast had been heard by Tim Selmer, call sign WA9SRW, a ham radio operator in Kewaunee, Wisconsin. Both Tim and Fred Richter were in contact with the news media in their respective states. Everyone had been on standby all afternoon waiting for word as to my whereabouts. Tim alerted the Coast Guard; Fred Richter called my Dad and the news media about my signal. At the time, I was not aware of any of this. Once I had confirmed I was actually seeing the flashing light from Manitowoc, I stopped my radio navigation and simply steered toward the beacon.

As the darkness grew, so did my awareness of lights on the shore. I was definitely making progress toward Manitowoc when another horrifying thought struck me. Here I was, moving along a few miles offshore without any lights! I began keeping a wary eye out for any other boats. What an ignominious ending to be hit by an unsuspecting boat this close to completing the trip.

By this time the sun had fully set and the night sky was in full bloom. The shoreline lights of Two Rivers, Wisconsin, eight miles to the north of Manitowoc, were now in full view, and it was a spectacular and unforgettable sight. Fortunately, the ambient light let me continue to switch fuel hoses without incident. I had not planned on having enough fuel to still be running after dark, so I didn't have any lights rigged on the tub. However, I had brought along two emergency flares. I planned on saving these until I ran out of fuel. The light from the flares lasts for many minutes and just might be seen by someone on shore.

Time seemed to stand still. My trip was now an all-out race of distance versus fuel. I could make out the lighthouses on the ends of the breakwaters at the Manitowoc harbor entrance. Excitement was building because I knew that at any moment the motor might sputter to a stop and my quest to cross the Lake would be over. I was now switching fuel hoses after only a minute or two, trying to get the last ounces out of each tank.

Suddenly, out of the darkness, as I peered toward the channel between the breakwaters, a large buoy loomed directly ahead and only a few yards away. I made a very sharp turn, with only inches to spare, to avoid a collision with this floating monster. That near disaster forced me into high alert for anything else floating out there in the darkness between me and the Manitowoc shore. Off in the distance on the south breakwater, I could now see what appeared to be a large flock of birds. As I got closer, I realized that it wasn't birds. It was people, gobs of people! By now I was only a few hundred yards from the breakwater entrance. I began to wonder what those people were doing out there on the breakwater this late in the evening. The fishing must really be great. It never occurred to me they were looking for an overdue bathtub sailor.

I had seen the lights of a boat or two passing out of the channel between the breakwater when I was a mile or so away, and I was really worried about a collision with a speeding boat that couldn't see me. I wasn't sure that I could get out of the way fast enough. The thoughts of a possible collision with a speeding boat, my near miss of a buoy a few minutes before, and the threat of imminent fuel starvation kept me very alert and focused as I approached the Manitowoc harbor entrance channel in the dark.

I had been on the water for more than 14 hours and the constant pressure was taking its toll. But there was Manitowoc, my goal, in sight! In a minute or two, if the outboard motor continued to run, if I didn't hit anything and nothing hit me, I would make it to the Manitowoc harbor entrance. The excitement of the moment was building as I clung to my last shreds of energy and the limits of my abilities and luck.

The trials and tribulations of the day suddenly faded in the adrenaline rush of excitement as I passed between the lighthouses and through the entrance into the Manitowoc harbor. A thousand new thoughts were suddenly swirling in my mind. I was jubilant beyond words! Ineffable joy! I realized that my life would never be the same again. The most satisfying thought was the anticipation of being able to face the people who said it couldn't be done. What a relief to be able to shed the badge of failure. I had done it! Fair and square. On my own, no matter what happened, the fact was made. I had done it! I still get shivers thinking about the sheer audacity of that moment.

I was close to the north seawall when I noticed a lone Coast Guardsman standing a few feet away. He was obviously dispatched to look for the missing bathtub. He was very interested in my craft and shouted to me inquiring if I was all right. I shouted back that I was just fine, but where could I get some fuel since I didn't think I had enough to make it to the municipal boat ramp, wherever that was. I was so busy shouting to the Coast Guardsman that I didn't notice a boat pull alongside. The two men must have heard me describing my lack of fuel. They immediately produced a gas can with a hose exactly like the one I had been using. As they passed it over, they eagerly told me to follow them to the municipal boat ramp. "The mayor and half the town are waiting for you," they yelled. I was very thankful to have a lighted escort to cross the dark harbor.

22

I did it! Arrival in Manitowoc

I have a vague recollection of a shouting, moving mass of people as I neared the municipal boat ramp. Moving slowly, I was directed to a certain location; questions were being shouted at me from all directions. A policeman on the dock arranging a tie-down finally told me to stop. Now my concern was for my bathtub craft and the practical problem of what would happen next. In all of my planning, plotting, daydreaming, and preparations for this venture, I had not anticipated or even imagined this mob scene of confusion and lights flashing in the darkness. I had always imagined that I would arrive in Manitowoc in bright daylight and be able to wave to people on shore and make a landing at some ramp in a dignified and proper manner. Instead, it was completely dark. I was directed to tie up at an unfamiliar dock, not a boat ramp.

And there were people everywhere, all crowding around to take flash pictures and catch a glimpse of the bathtub and the arrival.

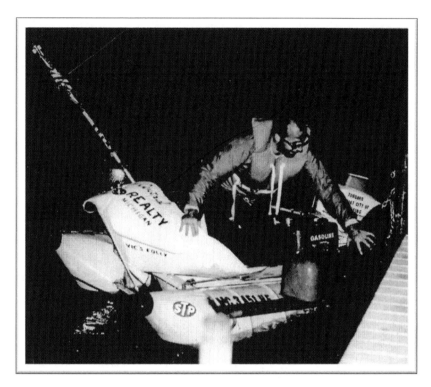

Photo by United Press International.

Above me on the dock, a man in Bermuda shorts was ordering some police officers to clear a path so I could disembark from the tub onto the dock. As I grabbed for a piling to pull myself up, a flashbulb went off in my face. For a few moments, everything around me was a veil of black nothingness; groping for a handhold on the wooden dock structure was difficult at best. Having just spent the last 14 hours in a semi-reclining position on a water and fuel-soaked mat, my body was a mass of objecting muscles. I used an old tire chained to the dock to pull myself and the free-floating tub close enough to climb out while holding my tie-down rope. Fortunately, there were several eager bystanders who facilitated my exit maneuver and a policeman grabbed the rope so Vic's Folly would not float away. Apparently, the officer was also there to make sure no one took any 'souvenirs' out of the bathtub.

After finally getting onto the dock, I was still pretty shaky in the legs, and I was not seeing or hearing too well what with all the flashing lights and shouting humanity. Between the flashbulbs going off and the flashlights being directed at my face, I was unable to see who was greeting me or even what was going on around me. Mayor John Krey was very gracious and welcomed me to the City of Manitowoc, Wisconsin.

Polaroid Photo given to Vic Jackson by an anonymous person
August 24, 1969

Now, the practical problems of a celebrity bathtub sailor started to crop up. Here I was the center of attention of a large crowd of people with reporters crowding around firing questions at me. The Mayor of Manitowoc was posing with me for pictures. Unknown to them, my biggest concern at that moment was how soon I was going to get to visit a restroom.

In planning for a trip of this nature, there were more than a few special issues that no one would ever think about unless they had done it before. For instance, if I did get across the lake,

I needed shoes and clothing for an overnight stay. The worst problem was a personal one. There was no restroom on Vic's Folly. My solution to this problem turned out to be simple, unique, and quite accidental. I simply 'held it' for the whole 14-hour trip! I was 31 years old, very healthy, and I didn't drink anything during the whole voyage. To this day, 50 years later, I don't know how I did it.

After a few minutes of conversation with the Mayor and the news media, I finally got the chance to indicate my desire to visit a restroom and freshen up a bit. However, before I could go anywhere, I needed to put my shoes on. Before getting in the tub at Ludington, I had carefully taken off my shoes and socks and placed them in the plastic garbage container. I discovered that although I had worn a jacket and long pants all day, my feet had been exposed to the sun. I had a devil of a time putting my socks and shoes on over the sunburn. Walking was a painful experience.

The mayor finally suggested that he would like to take me to dinner at a nearby restaurant. This was a fine idea, but another problem occurred to me. What was going to happen to the bathtub while we were gone? There was still a throng of people crowding around on the dock, trying to get a closer look at the famous bathtub. I was afraid for its safety. Mayor Krey quickly arranged for a police escort for the craft. He also arranged to have it towed through the channel to the bridge just down the river in downtown Manitowoc so that the bridge tender on duty all night could keep watch over it.

I had been on Lake Michigan all day; I had fought numerous problems and gone through one crisis after another since very early that morning; now the Mayor of Manitowoc and various other dignitaries wanted me to eat a rather formal dinner with them in a fancy restaurant with the entire place in an uproar over the celebrity bathtub sailor. It was a very generous and thoughtful gesture, but eating was difficult with everyone watching my every movement. I was also still wearing the same clothes that had soaked in the brackish water of the bathtub all day and the same gasoline-oil stained, fishy-smelling jacket. I remember drinking an extraordinary amount of water during dinner, but I have no memory of the food I ate. That memory was lost in the barrage of questions, answers and comments. Was I afraid? What happened to my radio? Where was I when everyone was looking for me?

The answers were simple and obvious, but I had trouble explaining the intricacies of bathtub sailing given my fatigue-fogged brain and my personal discomfort knowing I looked and smelled like a storm-rescued fisherman who badly needed a shower.

I was told my travels on the lake earlier in the day had even managed to disrupt local law enforcement. The shoreline road between Two Rivers and Manitowoc that Sunday afternoon was so heavily traveled with vehicles that the sheriff's department had to send extra officers to direct traffic. It seemed as though everyone in that part of Wisconsin was on the lookout for the missing bathtub, hoping they might spot the weird craft offshore in the big lake.

Finally, at what must have been past 11 p.m., Mayor Krey drove me to a hotel in downtown Manitowoc and checked me in for the night. Needless to say, I didn't need a bellhop to carry my luggage. I didn't have any. Mayor Krey told me that he would meet me for breakfast in the morning. I immediately climbed into bed after the most unusual day in my life, but I couldn't fall asleep. The events of the day kept replaying in my mind. Green, cascading water and howling wind and laughing crowds of people shouting strange things whirled around and around as I tried to fall asleep.

23

Facing the Press

I woke up at the crack of dawn wondering where I was. I had to get up and check out the window to get my bearings. Then I remembered yesterday.

That's when I decided to walk down to the bridge across the Manitowoc River to retrieve clean socks and check on the condition of the bathtub. It was still safely tied up below the bridge tender's shack. The only clothes I had were the same pants and jacket I wore crossing the lake, but at least I had clean socks. The bridge tender was a little surprised to see someone wanting access to the bathtub craft, but he instantly recognized me as the owner and let me make a quick check of the rig. Everything was in order.

As Mayor Krey and I were having breakfast that morning, he mentioned that he would like to formally present me with the key to the city at his office in a couple of hours. I was not the least bit bothered by having to wear the same smelly clothing to these planned events that I had worn the day before. Apparently, neither was the Mayor. He would send a car around to pick me up. We also discussed arrangements for the tub to be towed to the municipal launch ramp. A front-end loader would then pick up the whole rig and carry it from the municipal ramp around through downtown, across the channel to the C&O Carferry dock on the south side of the outer harbor. The famous bathtub craft and I could then ride the 1 p.m. City of Midland Carferry back to Ludington.

Newspaper headline:
"Bathtub Sailor Wins Bet"
with a sub headline:
"Conquers Lake Michigan"
Lansing State Journal
August 25, 1969, Lansing, Michigan

A few minutes before 10 that morning, a car arrived to take me to the city offices in Manitowoc. I was escorted into a small office. I assumed that the Mayor had arranged to have the local newspaper take our picture together as he presented me with the key to the city and that after a few words we would proceed with his plan to transport the bathtub rig to the carferry dock.

After a few minutes in the empty office, I was escorted through a door and up to a lectern crowded with microphones in a large room filled with what seemed like every television, radio and newspaper reporter in the state. I was flabbergasted! It was like a presidential-scale news conference, and I was the main attraction. In an official ceremony, the Mayor of Manitowoc presented me with the key to the city and made a few remarks about the importance of Lake Michigan and visitors to the Wisconsin shore community. Then the news media representatives had their chance to question the bathtub sailor.

The reporters were full of questions, questions, and more questions. I quickly learned to watch my mouth and mind my manners because every word and every gesture was being recorded for possible later broadcast. In the course of questioning, I mentioned that I had come mighty close to running out of fuel. In fact, I said, toward the end, I was able to pick up any of the six-gallon fuel cans (which when full weighed about 37 pounds) with two fingers and a thumb, much as one would pick up a cup of tea. One of the reporters then asked if I could show them exactly how much fuel I had left in the tanks. The media wanted to see the results for themselves. So, it was quickly arranged that we would all go en-masse to the municipal launch ramp to examine the bathtub rig and I would check the fuel quantity on camera. After a few more photos, we all adjourned to the municipal launching ramp near downtown Manitowoc.

With several TV cameras going, I emptied all five of the fuel containers into a clear glass fruit jar. I had a total of about one pint left. It was an impressive display of just how close I came to disaster. The reporters expressed great amazement at how little fuel was left. I was surprised there was that much. It was obvious that a whole bunch of luck and good fortune had been with me on the previous day's trip.

About this time, a front-end loader arrived and after much grunting and groaning a chain went around the rig and it was picked up in the bucket. It was then driven through the city streets and delivered to the C&O Carferry dock, thanks to the City of Manitowoc.

The freight clerk at the C&O dock in Manitowoc was somewhat confused as to what or how he was supposed to charge for my unusual craft. Was it to be considered a vehicle or a piece of freight? He finally settled on it being a piece of freight and asked how much it weighed. We guessed it to be 300 pounds. My prior planning had not included the details or possible costs of how the bathtub rig would get back to Michigan. Fortunately, I had my wallet because the freight charge for the bathtub rig was $30. The C&O ticket agent, trying for some humor, told me and my entourage that the alternative if I couldn't come up with the money would be to fuel up the tanks and run it back across the lake the same way it came. They were only joking, but it was probably a good thing Fred Behnke wasn't there to bet me another five dollars on a return trip to Ludington.

After approximately 24 railroad cars and 50 automobiles were loaded aboard, several of the deck hands and I hand-carried the heavy rig onto the fantail of the 406-foot City of Midland Carferry just ahead of the sea gate. It was a strange and unusual sight. For many years afterward, tourists could see displayed in the passenger lounge a snapshot of the bathtub rig sitting in all its glory on the fantail of the big ship.

Finally, after all the excitement of the previous day and a half, I could look forward to a leisurely four hours of relaxation without reporters or gawking crowds or life-threatening situations. So, as the ferry steamed out through the channel and got on course for the return trip to Ludington, I made my way up to the bow area where lounge deck chairs allowed me to stretch out and close my eyes for a little rest. After settling down for a few minutes, I suddenly became aware of a presence above me. Several boys were standing next to my deck lounger hovering over my head. When I opened my eyes they immediately asked if that was my bathtub craft on the rear car deck. Without thinking of the consequences, I said "yes." They immediately thrust out paper placemats from the ferry's dining room and asked if I would autograph them. I was dumbfounded. Me, autograph something? They handed me a pen and I dutifully signed their placemats. This activity immediately caught the eye of everyone else on the foredeck, and within seconds I was again facing a crowd of questions, autographs, handshakes, and general pandemonium. There were at least 200 passengers on the boat that afternoon, and it seemed like they were all around me. Chaos reigned for a few minutes as I fended off the questions and the requests for autographs. Fame was becoming a burden. Mysteriously, a ship's deckhand quietly appeared at my side. He said that I should accompany him up to the pilot house because the captain wanted to see me. I figured I was in big trouble now because of all the commotion and ruckus I had caused. When I arrived at the door to the pilot house, the Captain, Ernest "Gus" Barth, had a big smile on his face and welcomed me in. He explained that it looked like I was in need of relief from the crowd and I was welcome to spend my time in the pilot house, which was off limits to regular passengers. Besides, he had a few questions about that bathtub himself.

It was interesting to note that as we passed another carferry traveling west in the middle of the lake, the ship's radio came alive with a question from the passing ship as to whether the bathtub craft was on board. The comment was relayed that there were more than a few curious people in Ludington anxious to see the now successful, famous bathtub.

The ferry dock in Ludington was a busy place. I had to have the snowmobile trailer brought around to the fantail to load the bathtub; this was not an easy operation because of its weight. Normally, it was floated onto the snowmobile trailer from the water. The whole operation was done in record time, however, because everyone else on the ferry was waiting for me to get off the ship so that they could get off.

I spent only a short time in Ludington that Monday afternoon. I had to return to East Lansing so that I could get back to my work routine on Tuesday morning. Notoriety and fleeting fame had to take a back seat to activities that involved a paycheck.

Paul Harvey made amends for his earlier comments when he again mentioned on his Monday afternoon broadcast: Remember the man trying to cross Lake Michigan in a bathtub, (pause) "He did it!"

Newspaper headlines:
"Vic's Folly makes it across Lake"
Ludington Daily News
August 25, 1969, Ludington, Michigan

"Bathtub Sails Safely Across Lake Michigan"
Pensacola News Journal
August 25, 1969, Pensacola, Florida

On Wednesday, August 27, all of the Jackson kids made the front page of the Lansing State Journal in its afternoon edition. After being associated with a famous failure all summer, the children of the bathtub sailor finally were able to bask in some semblance of exultation. "Vic's Folly" had returned home.

Four days later, the Mayor of Lansing, Michigan, Gerald Graves, presented me with a Proclamation declaring Friday, August 29, 1969 as "Victor Jackson Day" in the City of Lansing. It was a bonus payback for all the humiliation and public derision I had suffered over the preceding months. Now I could go on with life and living in a new world where I may be looked upon as a crazy man, but a successful one nonetheless.

City of LANSING

LANSING, MICHIGAN

GERALD W. GRAVES, MAYOR

PROCLAMATION

WHEREAS: Victor Jackson has contributed untold numbers of hours in search for means and modes of new transportation by personally converting a steel bathtub into a water power craft; and

WHEREAS: He has offered unlimited advances in the highly complicated field of Marine research by the unprecedented bathtub voyage across Lake Michigan on Sunday, August 24, 1969; and

WHEREAS: Through pure personal courage, he has both created and conquered a seemingly unsurmountable challenge by successfully journeying from Ludington to Manitowoc, Wisconsin; and

WHEREAS: Victor Jackson has braved the strong and dangerous sea and has come safely home to shore to rejoice with family, friends and well-wishers;

NOW, THEREFORE, I, GERALD W. GRAVES, by the power vested in me as the Mayor of the City of Lansing, do proclaim, Friday, August 29, 1969, as

"VICTOR JACKSON DAY"

in Lansing and do heartily commend to all our citizens a full participation in all events related thereto in this community.

Given under my hand and the Seal of the City this twenty-fifth day of August, in the year of our Lord one thousand nine hundred and sixty-nine.

Gerald W. Graves
Mayor

Photo by Vic Jackson

24

Fame and Celebrity

After a tumultuous summer, I wanted nothing more than to settle into my familiar work routine at Troup Electronics. But fame was still complicating my life, and it emerged from unfamiliar places. Various schemes for fame and fortune by opportunists continued to arrive at my home for some weeks. I was invited to participate in a charity bathtub race across the Maumee River in Maumee, Ohio. I accepted this challenge, but it was no race. My bathtub was far better equipped than the other entrants, and I won easily. There was only a trophy as the winner's prize, but it was great fun.

One evening in mid-September a lady called and claimed she was a representative from Goodson-Todman Productions in New York, wanting to know if I would agree to appear on the television panel show "To Tell The Truth," starring Garry Moore. I was skeptical of the call because of all the other questionable things I had been 'invited' to do since the successful bathtub trip. I told the caller that if she was serious to send me the airline tickets. To my surprise a few days later an envelope containing a first-class airline ticket to New York arrived.

In order to provide some pictures for the show's producers, I had a professional photographer take a series of close-up photographs of the craft from all angles. The TV people chose only one photo of the bathtub craft, as might be expected for such a show. I kept the rest of the pictures just in case I ever wanted to build another bathtub boat. Besides, conversation is never dull in the presence of pictures of my bathtub.

Below is one of the pictures demonstrating how one rides in "Vic's Folly"; this photo was not used on the show.

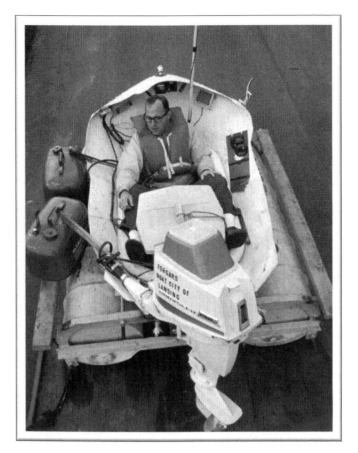

Photo by Paul Zarkovich

Going to New York City as a quasi-celebrity was a once in a lifetime experience for me. I was taken to eat at place where the bill for lunch for two people was more than I made in wages in one week. Being backstage in a New York network television studio and going through a rehearsal for the panel show were impressive events to a country bumpkin from East Lansing, Michigan.

When it came time for taping the show, two impersonators and I were sent on stage to each in turn answer the question, "What is your name?"

Then, host Garry Moore announced, "Here is Victor Jackson's fresh- water fable as follows." He proceeded to read this statement:

"I, Victor Jackson, sailed across Lake Michigan in a most unusual boat. Her name is "Vic's Folly" and is powered by a 20-horsepower outboard motor. The first day I attempted my historic voyage I was swamped by six-foot high waves and had to turn back. On the day I finally completed my epic journey the battery on my radio went completely dead and I was down to one pint of gas before I sighted land. Although Vic's Folly is officially registered as a one passenger pleasure craft, I believe most people would immediately recognize it as a common, garden variety, cast iron bathtub. Signed, Victor Jackson"

The celebrity panel consisted of Kitty Carlisle, a well- known television personality and New York newspaper columnist; Orson Bean, a comedian and actor; Bill Cullen, a well-known television host and panelist; and, Pat Carroll, a movie, television and stage actress. After questions from the panel directed to the two impersonators, who could say anything they wanted, and to myself, who had to tell the truth, the celebrity panel voted for the person they thought was the real Victor Jackson, the man who had taken a bathtub across Lake Michigan. All four votes from the panel went to my impersonators: Jack Davis a vice-president of a jewelry company, and Bill Frost, a social director of a honeymoon resort. By the rules of the show, the two impersonators and I were each awarded a $500 prize. When the taping was over, we were instructed to meet the panel members on stage as part of the closing scene of the show. Fortunately, no audio recording from the stage was made during this informal meeting. Kitty made a beeline to where I was standing and peered at me at close range over her reading glasses. Without a second thought, she blurted out: "You just don't look like that kind of a nut to me." Then Garry Moore expressed his amazement that my bathtub was smaller than the dinghy on his sailboat. You never know what words will come out of the mouths of entertainers.

The trip to New York was a memorable experience that was practice for one last fling at fame. I was contacted by a booking agent wanting to know if I was interested in going on the boat show tour circuit around the country. The contract would last for a year of weekend shows. The offer was quite attractive, but I couldn't figure out what a bathtub sailor would do after the year was over.

In a last fling at celebrity, I agreed to be the featured attraction at the Cincinnati, Ohio Boat Show in January 1970. Although my bathtub watercraft was more of a raft or barge than the speedboats and fishing outfits that were on display, the bathtub craft vividly demonstrated that an old-fashioned cast iron bathtub can be made to float, but you probably don't want to attempt to cross Lake Michigan in it.

Photo by Paul Zarkovich

In the big picture of life however, the real payoff for all of the agony, ridicule, danger and knuckle-headed persistence expended in the name of a bizarre quest, was a personal triumph that changed my life for the better, and showed the world that anyone can accomplish anything if he or she truly believes they can.

It was a memorable summer of 1969 in many ways. It was a conjunction of odds and ends, humor and danger, lows and highs. There was fleeting fame, but no great monetary wealth associated with the bathtub adventure. Now all that's left after all these many years are a few mementos and a fantastic story for the grandchildren and great grandchildren that ends with an exclamation point. "Yes, your old grandpa really, really did go across Lake Michigan in a bathtub!"

25

Requiem for a Bathtub Boat

When winter 1970 arrived in full force, it was time to return all the borrowed equipment that had made the bathtub a successful voyager. Before returning Dick Cahill's trailer for his snowmobiles, I asked my sister Gail if I could store the bathtub behind her garage in Eastlake until I could decide what to do with it.

Some 20 years later, I still had not made up my mind, most of the barrels had rusted away, and the whole thing was junk. Brother-in-law Art Breece contacted me to see what I wanted to do with the old rig, but I could only suggest the dump as a final resting place. My teenage nephews Kenny and Jay Breece were very disappointed to see the old rig hauled away because they could entertain friends for hours either sitting in the old tub or telling wild stories about it. Some of those stories may not have been too far from the truth. Since the tub was out behind the garage, they probably did a few other things in it too.

Art Breece told me that the bathtub itself became an animal feeding trough on a farm in Freesoil, Michigan, and the rest of the rusted-out hulk went to the Eastlake dump. What an ignominious end to a lively adventure! I am forever indebted to my brother-in-law for his storage services and patience dealing with a determined procrastinator.

The final chapter of the great bathtub venture took more than a little time.

On many fronts, 1969 was a tumultuous year for me. After returning from my adventures on Lake Michigan and in the television world, other life altering events occurred. In early October 1969, Everett Troup, owner of Troup Electronics died from a sudden heart attack. Shortly thereafter, Fred Behnke left Troup Electronics to climb the ladder in the communications field. Unfortunately, in all the commotion after returning from my Lake Michigan venture, I failed to collect the five-dollar bathtub bet from Fred, and we lost contact with each other in a world devoid of social media and email. As time and circumstance would have it, within a year I was also in a new job at a new company. The great bathtub venture became the subject of some entertainment for local service clubs and a wall decoration of odd memories and intriguing conversations, but nothing more. The original wager with Fred faded into the obscurity of everyday life and living.

In 1979, totally by chance, a friend asked if I would like to meet an old work mate for lunch. Lo and behold, who did I meet in a bar in Southfield? None other than Fred Behnke. Finally, after some reminiscing about our time at Troup Electronics Fred and I were able to have the conversation we had missed so many years before. I finally got around to officially demanding my five bucks. It was a rare opportunity to meet an old buddy and recall the good times and the wild stories.

When he finally got around to it, Fred very carefully opened his wallet and fished around for a five-dollar bill. Eventually, he found one and laid it out on the bar. Then, with a flourish, Fred Behnke signed his name and wrote Bathtrip Argument on the face. The original wager was finally paid off, in cash no less, and the last detail of the wild summer of 1969 was put to rest. That five-dollar bill is now a prized possession worth infinitely more than its face value.

Photo by Karen Jackson

By sheer coincidence, a few years after the bathtub bet was paid in full, Gary Barfknecht's 1982 book, Michillaneous, and his 1984 book, Mich-Again's Day listed the bathtub trip as a "Fantastic Voyage" among the notable things associated with Michigan.

But, hold on, this story is not quite finished. In the summer of 2016, some 47 years after the amazing bathtub voyage, the Jackson's held a family reunion picnic. The bathtub story comes up frequently at these gatherings. Everyone—grown children, grandchildren, great grandchildren, aunts, uncles, and cousins—wants to know: What happened to the bathtub?

I repeated my aged and decrepit memory that, as far as I knew, some 30 years ago, more or less, the bathtub became a barnyard fixture on the farm of a relative of my now deceased brother-in-law, Art Breece, in the village of Freesoil, Michigan. Art's daughter, Linda, and her husband Bruce Shannon, who live in Eastlake, about 20 miles from Freesoil, listened attentively to the conversation.

A few months later, Linda and Bruce's daughter Janelle and husband Kevin came to Lansing to drop off their son Brandon for his induction into the Air Force. We met the group for dinner at a restaurant in Lansing, and when the meal was finished they invited me out to the parking lot to see Brandon's brand new truck. And what a mind-boggling surprise I got!

Lying in the shiny new pickup's bed was a very battered and very old cast iron bathtub that still had the remains of a transom board in the rear and drilled holes in the front and back rim that positively identified it. Vic's Folly, the once famous bathtub, had been returned to me after almost 50 years. No small feat, thanks to the significant efforts of Bruce Shannon, who had scoured the farm's barnyard, as described in family lore, and reclaimed the ancient mariner as a long-lost heirloom. It had served as a water trough and large animal feeder for many years.

The newly reclaimed vessel has generated somewhat of a dilemma for an 81-year-old man of proven weirdness. What exactly does a person do with an old, but famous, bathtub? Plant flowers in it? Make a really uncanny yard decoration? Create the world's smallest museum collection of famous old bathtubs?

The old and battered "Vic's Folly" bathtub is currently housed in a garage where it is being reconstructed for display purposes. It has been suggested by some that it belongs in a real museum. My children, Victor "Lee" Jr., Kevin, Wendy, Kelly, Gene, Robin, Kerry, and Jody will happily donate the reconstructed "Vic's Folly" to a suitable museum, assuming of course that the museum actually wants this world-famous relic of faded memories and fantastic voyages.

About the Author

At age 81, Vic Jackson is an active outdoorsman who loves a challenge. In addition to "bathtub boating", as a young man he also walked a one-day 50-mile hike in below zero-degree Fahrenheit weather. Vic is currently an avid bicyclist who has peddled thousands of miles throughout the United States, including Alaska and Hawaii.

Vic is mostly retired from his career as an engineer, technician, communications system owner and consultant. During his career, he founded several successful telecommunications companies. He is a licensed instrument rated commercial pilot and has enjoyed hobbies that include amateur radio (call sign W9NDM, and former W8BLP), running, flying, golfing, motorcycling, and fishing.

Vic lives with his wife, Karen Jackson in Okemos, MI and boasts a combined family of 9 children, 8 grandchildren and 5 great-grandchildren.